Growing Up Stoned

COMING TO TERMS WITH TEENAGE DRUG ABUSE IN MODERN AMERICA

by Dan C. Ellis

Published by
Health Communications, Inc.
1721 Blount Road, Suite 1
Pompano Beach, Florida 33069

ISBN 0-932194-35-4

Printed in the United States of America

For my daughter Abby,
from whom
I have learned so much
of what I know
and
to whom
I am ever grateful.

Contents

Introduction

When I started working with chemically dependent adolescents, I quickly realized there were few guide markers. I made many mistakes, but did not give up and, as a result, learned what not to do. As I contemplated writing this book, I thought of those things I wish I had known when I began working with adolescents. This book is not only a summary of what I have learned, but of the knowledge and experience of many other clinicians who have also struggled with the adolescent client.

Although I believe that chemical dependency is a disease process, I have come to learn that it is also a developmental disorder. Adolescent development is difficult enough, and the addition of drugs will only make it worse. It seemed time to write one book about dependency and development in the adolescent. This book offers a "model" which views treatment from both a therapeutic and developmental perspective. Chemical dependency is a serious adolescent problem which also tends to freeze, or even retard, normal development. Just getting kids sober is half the battle. The counselor must also be prepared to address the adolescent's developmental needs.

This book is not intended to be the complete source on adolescent development. Hopefully, the reader will be encouraged to do further reading on this subject. Competency comes from both experience and knowledge of this unique age group. Also, I hope the reader develops a sense of respect for adolescents and an understanding of what motivates them.

In the chapters that follow, the reader will notice that I have used the words "counseling" and "therapy" interchangeably. Also, I interchange gender references. This may offend some readers, and others may take no notice. I do not want to imply any particular importance to my various choices of terms.

The chemical dependency field progressively is having more impact on chemical dependency at earlier stages. This requires that the counselor be prepared to work with an ever-broadening range of clients. We are seeing younger and younger clients in treatment. These clients require new skills and knowledge of the counselor. Those counselors who do not advance their knowledge and skills will find it difficult to keep up.

Chapter 1

Understanding Adolescent Stages of Development

A Frame of Reference

Anyone who has spent time with, or has raised an adolescent, is likely to have formed definite opinions about them. These opinions will be influenced by whatever beliefs, values, expectations and stereotypes one possesses about adolescents. Experience, as well as social research, has shown that our pre-conceived notions have a great impact upon how we perceive our environment. If we expect to have a negative experience with a given group of people, then the odds are increased that we will. Although everyone was at one time an adolescent, this does not automatically grant us understanding. We may have had negative experiences as adolescents, or we may have only seen obnoxious behavior in the adolescents we have known. It was this author's notion, when first encountering adolescents professionally, that they were, by and large, an unruly, self-centered and hopelessly insane group who, fortunately, would outgrow their condition. It was believed that adolescents should be approached with caution, and one should be prepared to defend oneself if they should attack.

The concepts above proved to be inaccurate and totally unfair. However, the author had to look at himself and recognize that it was his perceptions which created the threat, not the adolescents themselves. It became necessary to learn to like and understand adolescents. Coming to appreciate young people's problems and viewpoints began to shed new light on the entire process of human development. The dynamics of adolescent growth became, for this author, a purposeful set of tasks and accomplishments leading the individual to a new level of consciousness and abilities. One cannot simply jump from childhood to adulthood; there must be a gradual transition while the psychic and physical person grows into the new adult form. Understanding this process is essential to being successful in treating the chemically dependent adolescent.

These predetermined notions and stereotypes we possess regarding adolescents can present a block, not only to parenting, but to therapy as well. When counselors first begin working with adolescents, they may find that they must set aside their prejudices (if possible), and re-develop a new "frame of reference." There must exist a willingness to re-think one's attitudes about adolescents before beginning to treat them. This chapter, and the remainder of the book, will offer helpful information, but readers must provide the desire to re-evaluate their beliefs.

The author has discovered that the clinician must also possess an attraction for this unique population of clients. Simply understanding adolescents, without an attraction to work with them, and personally appreciating their status in life, will not result in productive therapy. Too often the author has observed therapists trying to push adolescents through delicate stages of development too quickly. The therapist believes he will be more effective if he can bring the child to an adult level of functioning. This is a great disservice to the young person.

To further complicate things, an accepting attitude and attraction towards adolescents may not be enough to be an effective clinician. One must consider the adolescent's perception of the therapist. Does the adolescent find the therapist's attitudes and behaviors attractive and conducive to an open relationship? Do adolescents find you to be "OK," or do they find you to be "weird" and unapproachable? To be an effective clinician for the adolescent client, one must possess a frame of reference which lends him both competency and credibility.

This chapter will focus on understanding the unique stages of development this age group experiences as they attempt to give birth to a newly-independent human being.

In the field of human development, much has been done to clarify, catalog and characterize human growth and change. We seem to know the most about the earliest years of life—between infancy and about five years of age. We owe much of this knowledge to the work of Jean Piaget and Erik Erickson. Both theorists offer distinct developmental stages of growth from birth through death. However, both Piaget and Erickson conducted much of their research on the young child, and so the bulk of the literature concerns this age group. Children under the age of five are clearly easier to observe than the typical, active 13-year-old.

With adolescents, there exists a variety of theories, many of which possess common beliefs, as well as divergent opinions. In the past, many clinicians and theorists considered adolescence as a rather prolonged period of insanity, linking childhood with adulthood. Psychopathology and behavioral disturbances were considered to be normal and necessary to survive the libidinal sexual desires one was supposed to have for his/her mother or father. It now seems that adolescence is a distinct stage of development with its own specific tasks to be performed (Offer and Offer, 1973). Adolescence is a stage of life that begins with puberty (approximately 11 years of age), and ends when one has attained reasonable independence and psychological congruence (approximately 21 years of age).

It is often difficult to comprehend adolescents as having a specific task to perform, or anything of importance to do, beyond irritating the adults in their lives. Yet, this is generally an interpretation of behavior which we have determined that we do not like. Because we do not understand adolescent behavior, we may attribute bad motives to it. When we are confronted with such behaviors, we may believe they are intended to frustrate or infuriate us. However, the work of Erickson and Piaget has enabled us to overcome our tendency to attribute the worst to behavior we do not understand. Because adolescent behavior can present an outward appearance of disorganiztion and purposelessness, we can easily fail to understand the goals of such behavior. Actually, it is believed that most adolescent behaviors have rather simple motivations at their roots. Yet, without understanding, this simplicity can be hard to discern.

David Elkind has written a wealth of material on the contemporary adolescent (1978, 1980, 1983). Elkind explains that as the child enters the stage of formal operations (as identified by Piaget), he attains a new capacity to think. This new ability allows the adolescent to hold many variables in mind, while solving new, more complicated problems. Also, the early adolescent — 11-14 — can begin to conceive his or her own ideals, identify contrary propositions, understand metaphors and similes. Yet, as with any new-found skill, the youngster is not yet adept at these new, formal operations. The young adolescent cannot yet assign appropriate priorities to concepts and, at times, will miss the obvious while distracted by a "profound thought." They seek complex motivations where the most simple is, in fact, true. The need to be "right" can overwhelm the adolescent's judgment, and throw him into a bitter battle with friends, parents, or siblings over the most trivial matters. No wonder adolescents can be so adept at things like video games and "Trivial Pursuit." These activities provide an opportunity to focus one's concentration on something which, at the time, seems immensely important.

Elkind points out how each of us possesses an "imaginary audience" inside our heads. The adolescent's is exceptional. We have all observed an adolescent express the belief that everyone is watching him and laughing at some minor error he has committed. They have limited ability to understand that what is of interest to them may have relatively little importance to anyone else. But, because the adolescent can now think about other people's thinking, he is doomed to self-inflicted self-consciousness of the most severe degree. It does not occur to adolescents that their perception of others may be inaccurate, or distorted. The author is reminded of numerous occasions when his own daughter was embarrassed by her own thoughts, rather than what she believed to be the thoughts of others. This ability to distinguish between one's own thoughts and those of others is beyond the early adolescent. "If I think I did something stupid, then everyone else must think the same thing." Although early adolescents can conceive differing points of view about the same event, they seem unable to apply this principle to themselves.

It is common, then for adolescent behavior to emerge with an imaginary audience in mind. This phenomenon can be utilized to explain a good portion of adolescent vandalism and general acting-out in public. Vandalism often occurs with the reaction of the victim (even if they do not personally know the victim) in mind. "Boy, will they be mad when they see this mess!" This can also become a way for the adolescent to express unidentified anger. A similar process can be true when it comes to experimenting with drugs. If the child believes that the peer group values getting high, then there will be a strong inner urge to behave in a way pleasing to the group. "If I get high with my friends, then I am in compliance with their wishes for me, and this is pleasing to me." This kind of thinking allows the adolescent to avoid experiencing internal conflict with the peer group. However, getting high to avoid conflict with the perceived values of the peer group will put the person in conflict with other value systems, namely those of the parents. This desire to please that imaginary audience (peers), can drive adolescents to cross boundaries which heretofore they would not have crossed. The healthy adolescent generally experiments with drugs only to the degree which he believes will gain him the desired acceptance. The unhealthy, or pre-dependent, person may quickly lose control and continue to use drugs with increasing frequency, not to please the peer group, but to satisfy the urge to remain high.

Adolescents also tend to believe they are unique, and that no one else can understand them, nor has anyone ever experienced their particular predicament. Also, they may believe that they are outside of the normal "rules" of life, due to their uniqueness. Many parents have heard the plaintive plea, "But Mom, you just don't know what it is like to be in love." Or, "Others may grow old and die, but not me; others may become dependent on drugs, but not me; others may get pregnant, but not me." These egocentric ideas begin to go away as the adolescent matures and confronts reality in a more congruent manner. To think this way is not abnormal. However, some adolescents who become dependent upon drugs can get stuck in this phase long beyond what is appropriate. Rigid thinking can be characteristic of most adolescents, but the dependent person displays an extreme level of rigidity. The normal adolescent will argue his point intensely until he is presented with concrete facts to the contrary, and then simply submit—or revise his argument to fit the facts. The dependent adolescent, who is desperately trying to hide his use, may continue to argue long beyond what is reasonable, even in the face of contrary facts. The irrationality of the arguing is supported by the desire of the child to deny and conceal his drug use.

These newly-formed concepts in early adolescents allow them to see inconsistencies and injustices in adult behavior. Unfortunately, the adolescent does not yet possess the ability to put this knowledge into perspective. It is common for siblings to protest the unrighteous behavior of their brother, yet turn around and repeat the same offense. The young adolescent finds it difficult to accept that some rules are, in fact, arbitrary, and not consistently enforced. However, the adolescent may at time be arbitrary in adhering to the rules, such as the young person whose parents require an 11 p.m. curfew, but since he feels midnight is fair, then decides to follow his own rule.

For the adolescent, the expression of an idea is right next to fully realizing it. Young people believe that if they can conceive a high moral ideal, then they have, in fact, attained it. And so the adolescent is rarely impressed with the parental injunction, "You have to work for what you want." The adolescent has not yet achieved the ability to know the difference between having an idea and fully realizing it; he believes they are one in the same. This phenomenon probably explains the notion of "generation gap." The idealism of the young person clashes with the pragmatism of the adult. If we can understand this, then maybe we can become more empathetic with the adolescent's failure to follow through at times.

Comprehending what makes an adolescent "tick" does not always help us to "keep our cool" when dealing with him. Yet, it does help us if we can depersonalize some of their more bothersome behaviors. The young person can be in turmoil over the need to "individuate" (Blos, 1962) himself from perceived parental influence. And sometimes the adolescent may be abrasive, or reactionary, to a simple request. The therapist must view this outburst as an expression of internal conflict, and not over-react also.

This need to individuate can be expressed through efforts to put distance between oneself and the perceived threat of the loss of autonomy due to parental interference. The adolescent does not see his reaction as excessive, but a justified effort to maintain his fragile independence. This defense system is necessary, and is actually an indication of a normal adolescent attempting to grow up. The young person who complies with every adult wish is side tracking his natural needs to develop as an independent person. It is useful to take a closer look at the compliant young person. This person's sense of identity may be so poorly formed that he distrusts his own feelings and ideas over those of others.

Adolescents possess terrific abilities to cope with stress, either the self-inflicted, or that which befalls them from the external world. The individual may not always handle stress with "style;" he is still awkward and emotional. But generally after a short period of sulking, or a brief outburst, the adolescent will recover quite well. Consider the everyday stress of a changing intellectual capacity, to say nothing of the changes one's body is going through. Yet, most young people manage to handle these stresses realtively well. In fact, most adolescent development is not as traumatic as we may have believed. Some amount of sullenness, withdrawal and rudeness is characteristic of the ways adolescents cope with distress. Prolonged periods of such response may Indicate a more serious problem, or an impairment in the natural coping mechanisms (drug-affected).

A majority of adolescents, according to Offer and Offer (1973), actually experience stable developmental sequences of growth. The Offers refer to this as *continuous growth*, where the young person is supported by tolerant parents who understand the changes taking place. The home environment is favorable, in that it offers economic, social, and physical stability. These adolescents could be characterized has having strong egos, good coping skills, and an ability to recover quickly from minor setbacks. These people tend to move slowly and cautiously towards heterosexual relationships, and maintain a positive self-image, even in the face of failures.

Another group identified by the Offers is that group characterized by *surgent growth*. These individuals did not experience the same genetic/environmental advantages as the continuous growth group. Although this group shows good ego strength, they are more vulnerable to trauma and setbacks, and realize less support (consistency) from their parents. This group is more prone to anger and depression. Yet, in the long run, this group still manages to complete each stage of development in reasonable order and efficiency.

The final group is that of *tumultuous growth*. These individuals come from less-than-favorable backgrounds. The parents are either non-supportive, or absent. The parents are generally distracted by the intensity of their own needs, and are struggling just to survive. There is little or no awareness of the needs of their children. When these adolescents experience trauma, the tendency is to react out of proportion to the severity of the event. These individuals are characterized by insecurity, confused values, limited internal resources, and few meaningful relationships.

The majority of the adolescents studied by the Offers were found to be in the continuous and surgent growth groups. This seems to support the belief that most adolescents are well equipped to handle the stresses of life, even when the surrounding conditions are less than favorable. Other studies have shown that turmoil may not be as crucial to successful adolescent development as was originally believed.

In order to form a useful frame of reference for working with adolescents, the clinician needs to possess a clear sense of what is normal. What some have described as possibly pathological, is more frequently a normal process of human development. The task of treating the chemically dependent adolescent is intensely complicated, and requires a better-than-average understanding of development, intellectual capacities, social relationships, self-image, parent-child relationships, and many other issues. If one is contemplating working with this population, or is already doing so, it is recommended that he/she ask him/herself some essential questions. Why do I want to work with adolescents? What are my biases regarding this age group? How do I contrast the adolescent patient with the adult patient? Do I have an accurate image of a "normal" teenager? Do I even know one?

Building An Identity

Identity can be a difficult thing to define; some refer to it as a "sense," and "attitude," or a "self-image." Erik Erickson (1968) has provided some enlightenment on the subject of identity. Erickson views identity as a psychosocial task that begins with puberty (approximately), but is not exclusive to this age group, and completing this task can be a life-long process. (Marcia (1980) provides a helpful definition when he describes identity as "a self structure; an internal, self-structured, dynamic organization of drives, abilities, beliefs and individual history." A well-developed identity structure is characterized by increased awareness of one's own uniqueness, as well as the similarities found in others. Knowing one's strengths and weaknesses further contributes to an integrated self identity. A less developed identity structure leads to confusion about one's own distinctiveness, and a limited ability to independently evaluate oneself.

Experience has demonstrated that adolescents have intense difficulties with this task of developing an identity. They are experiencing a period which is more crucial than most developmental periods, because there is a significant structural change occurring. It is a period of transition in cognitive tasks from concrete to formal operations. it is a time of challenge; a challenge of the old parent-influenced beliefs, and a drive towards newly developing personal and separate beliefs. Marcia views children moving from an industry-dominated stage (skill building), to the identity stage (secure sense of self), and finally to the intimacy stage (vulnerability to others). Building an identity is a process of negation and affirmation. The child must relinquish the parents as psychosexual objects, and their identity as "takers" of the parental values. During later adolescence, the person must also relinquish the fantasies of an idealized, glamorous lifestyle, and settle for something more down to earth. The drug-abusing adolescent may have serious difficulty in letting go of his idealized view of the self. His drug-induced state alters reality, and the adolescent may become dependent upon this distortion.

There is some evidence indicating that adolescent girls develop their identities in a slightly different order than do boys. Girls seem to place more importance in fulfilling their needs for intimate relationships first, rather than self-identity. Girls are more inclined to want to feel close and personal with their friends, where boys seem more interested in feeling competent in their self identity.

This developmental process tends to get accomplished slowly, and in bits and pieces; decisions are made and changed almost daily in a seemingly unending state of confusion. And so it frequently seems that adolescents are obsessed with posturing and external appearances. Yet, gradually a more consistent core, or structure, begins to emerge. Parent-child relationships are extremely influential during this process, because it is from this base that the adolescent initiates the task of identity development. The parenting style (Enright, 1980) seems to have a significant influence on the type of identity an adolescent may form. Enright and Elder (1962, 1963) have identified three styles of parenting:

Autocratic: The youth is not permitted to express his/her views on issues concerning him/her, or to take initiative in self-regulation.

Democratic: The adolescent is encouraged to freely contribute to the discussion and solution of relevant issues, but ultimate responsibility for the discussion remains with the parents.

Permissive: The adolescent has a more influential role in making decisions on matters which concern him/her than do the parents.

These three styles are based on a power continuum, with autocracy representing the most parental power. Generally, adolescent autonomy is negatively related to the level of parental power. The democratic parent tends to encourage more healthy autonomy, while the permissive parent encourages independence, but not responsibility and cooperation. The autocratic style does not tend to encourage autonomy, but rather compliance, or defiance. These three styles also contribute to four relatively distinct adolescent identity structures as defined by Marcia:

—Identity Achievement
—Foreclosure
—Identity Diffusion
—Moratorium

These constructs tend to become most identifiable by late adolescence, but the precursors can be traced back to early childhood. Parental attitudes and practices also have a strong influence upon the development of these identities.

Identity Achievements represent individuals who are experienced decision-makers (democratic parental influence) and are about to pursue self-chosen ideological positions and goals.

Foreclosures are characterized as those who are also committed to specific goals and ideological positions, but they have been selected by the parents (autocratic parental influence), rather than self-chosen. However, the foreclosures seem content with this situation until they are presented with ambiguity, and the parents are not available for guidance. This usually results in conflict and intense cognitive dissonance.

Identity Diffusion youth are representative of those with no set goals, or ideological direction, regardless of whether or not they may have experienced a decision-making period (permissive parents).

Moratoriums are individuals who are currently struggling with goals and/or ideological issues; they are in an identity crisis (autocratic or inconsistent parents).

When measuring for a tendency toward anxiety, Moratoriums and Foreclosures are generally found on the high end of the scale. When presented with pre-arranged ambiguous situations, the Moratoriums and Foreclosures experienced the most difficulty with decision-making (Marcia, 1967). The Identity Achievements and Identity Diffusions experienced the least anxiety. Identity Diffusions were familiar with ambiguity, and did not find it particularly stressful.

When looking at self-esteem, the Identity Achievements and Moratoriums are the most secure and last influenced by outside forces, whereas the Foreclosures and Identity Diffusions are more likely to alter their sense of self-esteem, depending upon external feedback.

Foreclosures and Identity Diffusions are the most endorsing of authoritarian values, and also tend to present more conventional and traditional moral values. The Identity Achievements and Moratoriums are more flexible and evaluative when it comes to moral values. It seems the Identity Achievements are most successful at sorting out their own values through an introspective and critical process, leading to a self-assured conclusion. Moratoriums seem to reach their conclusions through a more rebellious and reactionary process, actually choosing the opposites of perceived parent values.

Regarding autonomy, the Foreclosures and Identity Diffusions seem to be most insecure and most influenced by external feedback from others. The Identity Achievements and Moratoriums are more secure in their autonomy, and less influenced by others. The Foreclosures are more willing to involve their families in their decision-making, and will typically follow whatever advice is given. Identity Achievements take more personal responsibility for their own decisions, yet might consult their parents for guidance. The Moratoriums also take more responsibility for their decisions, but do not typically seek out parental guidance. The Identity Diffusions seem to wander in ambiguity over decision-making, and are not sure where to turn for advice. These people may, in fact, be prone to indiscriminately selecting unhelpful sources of advice. Their inability to determine bad advice from good advice puts them at risk for multiple problems. These children are at higher risk for drug abuse, due to their diffuse identity boundaries, and the desire to please whatever group they are with.

When considering styles of cognition, we find that the Identity Achievements function best when dealing with difficult problems requiring reflective thought. The Foreclosures and Identity Diffusions tend to respond quickly and impulsively to these situations. The cognitive identity of Foreclosures is characterized by extreme simplicity, Identity Achievements and Moratoriums by complexity, and Identity Diffusions by extreme complexity (disorganization of thought).

When looking at drug use, we find that Foreclosures tend to be adamant about non-drug use (Dufrense and Cross, 1972). The Identity Achievements are freer about choosing to use drugs, as are the Moratoriums. However, the Moratoriums and Identity Diffusions demonstrate more difficulty in stopping their drug use, once they start. This would seem consistent with the notion that those individuals who have trouble with decision-making would also have difficulties in knowing they have made a poor decision. The Identity Diffusions would simply wallow in ambiguity, while the Moratoriums would steadfastly stand by their "right" to do as they please.

The Moratorium group can be characterized as those who put off any final, or congruent decision-making. They perceive the inconsistencies in the world with an intensely critical eye. Because they have so much trouble reconciling the inequities they see, they feel any commitments would tend to be hypocritical and a betrayal of the self. These young people experience the most conflict with authority figures, and are the least cooperative with adults. However, this group tends to maintain intense loyalties to the peer group, as long as their peers support their beliefs. It would seem that this group would be at highest risk for chemical dependency, followed closely by the Identity Diffusions.

Furthermore, the Moratorium group seems more volatile in nature, and inclined towards seeking attention in negative and destructive ways. They have a strong desire to appear attractive and visible, but primarily with the peer group in mind. It is not unusual for the Moratoriums to become "leaders" of the rebellious segment of the adolescent population. They thrive on intense relationships, and will quickly move on to a new one as soon as the old one becomes boring. Their interactions with others are characterized by ambivalence, competitiveness, and intense engagement and disengagement. The Moratoriums are struggling to free themselves from parental values, while, in contrast, the Foreclosures seem to be luxuriating in their close parent-child relationships. The Moratoriums would tend to be attractive to the Identity Diffusion group.

Considering parenting patterns and their influence upon adolescent identity, we find the Foreclosures participating in a "love affair" with their parents (Jordon, 1970, 1971). The Foreclosure families were the most task-oriented, and the fathers seemed to dominate their sons. The expression of emotions was not encouraged in these families. The Identity Diffusion youth seem to have ambivalent relationships with their parents, and commonly experience rejection and detachment, particularly from their fathers.

Moratoriums also seem to have ambivalent relationships with their parents, and are frequently engaged in a struggle to free themselves from their mothers. Moratoriums tend to see their parents as disappointed in them, or as disapproving (Schilling, 1975). The Moratorium family could be best characterized as in a struggle for autonomy, activity and self-expression. The Identity Achievements tend to see their parents in a more balanced way.

There seem to be some significant differences between boys and girls when it comes to identity development. Female identity development appears to be a far more subtle and complicated task. This may be because intimacy is valued more, and parental expectations are greater for girls in this area. Also, it is harder to establish clear markers along the way when considering female development. Boys, by nature, are trained to be more outward in their actions, where girls tend to be more inward. The predominant concerns of most girls are not with occupation and ideology. Rather, girls are concerned with the establishment and maintenance of interpersonal relationships. It seems that identity formation takes longer for women than for men, just as the establishment of intimacy takes longer for men.

When considering the influence of parents, for girls the mother seems to have the most significant impact upon identity, while for boys it is the father. Interestingly, Enright (1980) found that autocratic fathers promoted Identity Achievement in females, but not in males. Democratic fathers had the most positive influence upon male identities. Enright's study seems to indicate that parent gender also has a great deal to do with an adolescent's ability to experience Identity Achievement. When discussing sex differences, it seems that the female gets more of her autonomy characteristics from her father, while the mother influences the daughter's sense of security in interpersonal relationships.

A Struggle for Values

Understanding the content of adolescent values is important in the treatment of their problems. As adolescents develop, their ability to think abstractly in terms of general concepts, hypotheses and propositions, they also begin to distinguish between the thinking of self and others. This cognitive growth enables adolescents to entertain a wider range of alternatives from which personal, occupational, sexual and ideological commitments are made (Feather, 1980).

The relative difference between identity and values can be a subtle one, and when attempting to define the two, it seems that the use of similar phrases is almost unavoidable. One way to distinguish this subtle difference is to view identity as an image of the self, and one's values become a means of protecting and maintaining the self-image. Rokeach (1973) goes on to define values as standards that guide and determine action, attitudes toward objects and situations, ideology, presentation of self to others, evaluations, judgments, justifications, comparisons of self with others, and attempts to influence others. Finally, a value functions as a standard, or criteria, that guides thought and action in various ways. When organized into value "systems," they function as general plans which can be used to resolve conflicts, and as a basis for decision-making.

Anyone who spends time observing adolescent behaviors will notice that it appears their values are in a constant state of change. The only thing constant in their lives is that they are constantly changing. Adolescent value systems are very sensitive to cultural changes, and are always on the crest of the wave of social change. Adult values seem to be influenced by cultural changes as well, but adults are slower to adopt these changes. Adults are more evaluative, while adolescents will embrace a new value immediately if

they believe it is the "in thing" to do. No adolescent wants to be perceived as "out of it" when it comes to knowing the latest fad, hairstyle, or favorite pasttime. Our culture has also discovered the adolescent to be a newly-emerging "Super Consumer," and there are tremendous profits to be made by selling to them. This vulnerability in the adolescents' values make them an easy target for an ever-new line of products. Our culture, in effect, helps to continually speed up the process of changing values. What was new yesterday is no longer marketable today. Most adolescents do not want to be caught out of step, or out of style with what is currently in vogue.

One noticeable change in adolescent and cultural values is a rapid shift in what is deemed as appropriate behaviors for the two sexes. There seems to be a trend away from traditional, stereotyped sex roles, and towards more androgynous sex roles. This seems to be manifested most clearly through the popular music (punk, new wave, etc.) and fashions. Whether this is a temporary trend, or one that will last, remains to be seen. Generally speaking, we still find adolescent males assigning higher importance to values concerned with achievement and competence, whereas females place more emphasis on values relating to nurturance and affiliation.

During the adolescent years, there is an increasing need for close relations with others in the same age group, who can provide love, security, and support. The young person is looking to meet these needs outside of the home as a means to achieving autonomy. As adolescents press toward autonomy, they develop a respect for those who challenge adults. There is also a deep concern for the underdog, and this helps adolescents to express their own feeling of being in the outsider role in society. A Presidential panel on youth (Coleman et al., 1974) commented on the status of youth in our society:

> *Youth are segregated from adults by the economic and educational institutions created by adults; they are deprived of psychic support from persons of other ages— a psychic support that once came from the family; they are subordinate and powerless in relation to adults, and outsiders to the dominant social institutions. Yet, they have money, they have access to a wide range of communication and control of some, and they are relatively large in number. (p. 125)*

Whether they realize it or not, adolescents are expressing a particular value via the process of peer group socialization. Through this process, they begin to develop such additional values as empathy and loyalty. These newly-emerging values are still in the formative stages, and so the adolescent may not always be consistent in his expression. Baumrind (1975) has identified adolescent value constructs related to social behavior: friendly versus hostile; facilitative versus disruptive; obedient versus disobedient; controlled versus uncontrolled; active versus passive; and, individualistic versus suggestible. Baumrind believes each adolescent takes a stand on each construct, and this then orients him to a "way" of viewing and dealing with the world. As an example, acceptance of traditionalist values would assume that one had experienced a disciplined and strong family life, where adherence to adult authority was accepted. The alienated youth would be characterized as someone who rejected adult authority and may have grown up in a strict, rejecting and inconsistent home environment.

Adolescent values are clearly influenced by place and time. Developmental theorists must take this into consideration when describing developmental stages and values. Although the basic constructs offered by Baumrind may be consistent, the particular way in which adolescents manifest them will differ. Adolescent values of today can be quite different from what they were ten years ago. The process for building values seems to remain the same, but the content does not.

The development of moral values is very much related to cognitive abilities. The young person cannot move on to more complicated moral concepts until he has reached the appropriate intellectual capacity. This is where adolescents are frequently misunderstood by adults. Adults may not realize that Sally reacts to discipline so negatively because her cognitive abilities do not allow her to see the rationale behind it. The early adolescent's sense of morality is determined in large part by her belief that everything in life must be reciprocal and equal. Punishment should fit the crime and not be arbitrary. Adolescemts' intellectual capacity may limit their ability to clearly understand the intent behind the punishment, and only view it as unfair. This would be consistent with the adolescents' attempt to individuate themselves from parental control.

According to Piaget, moral growth requires that the child give up egocentrism for realism, and develop a concept of self as distinct from others who have their own independent perspectives. This shift occurs in interactions with peers, beginning in childhood, and extending into adolescence in two ways:

1. By growing older, children attain relative equality with adults and older children, which lessens their unilateral respect for them, and gives the children confidence to participate with peers in decisions about applying and changing rules on the basis of reciprocity. Rules are now seen as the result of cooperative efforts, and are subject to change.

2. When one interacts with peers, there is often a need to take alternate and reciprocal roles with them. The child thus becomes sensitized to the inner states that underlie the acts of others; this contributes, among other things, to the tendency to take others' intentions into account.

This process identified above can become delicate and quite complicated as the young person develops. Even though adolescents begin to appreciate the experiences of others, they are still at times tormented by their lingering egocentristic tendencies. The author can remember, as an adolescent, asking himself the question, "Why can I only feel my own feelings and think my own thoughts? Why can't I feel the feelings of others and think the thoughts of others?" This egocentristic view can block the adolescent from realizing that his thoughts and feelings are, in fact, quite similar to those of others.

Adolescents erect their value systems, they seem to be governed by an internal set of regulations, or inhibitions (Hoffman, 1980). Usually, these internal inhibitions are based on a desire to minimize anxiety and rejection. The young person tends to be most concerned about nonacceptance by his peers. Parents and other adults are important, but do not seem to cause as much potential anxiety. Adolescents appear to internalize values in three ways. The first type operates to inhibit anxiety. This type refers to the general expectation that people often, without necessarily being aware of it, assume that their actions are constantly under surveillance. In the extreme, this may reflect an irrational fear of abiquitous authority figures, or retribution by gods and ghosts. The result, in any case, is that the individual often behaves in the morally prescribed way, even when alone, in order to avoid punishment. The punishment may have, in fact, been real, or may only be perceived punishment.

Yet, this is an important distinction to note. The child who learns to control his behavior and values due to a fear of real punishment may not, in reality, be exhibiting true internalized control. This child may only be feigning internal control to avoid punishment he has experienced in the past. A real, yet primitive, form of internalization requires that anxiety over deviation be related to a sincere adoption of a particular value. In this case, external surveillance is unneccessary; the adolescent provides his own.

The second type of internalization process is an empathy-based concern for others. This second type pertains to the integration of the human capacity for empathy, and the cognitive awareness of other people's inner states. Adolescents learn that as they affect others through their behavior, they are alternately affected by them in similar ways. This process also helps to heighten the individual's sensitivity to the inner states aroused in others by one's own behavior. Having been in the other person's place helps one to know how the latter feels in response to one's behavior.

The final type of value internalization is the cognitive disequilibrium type. This type pertains to an adolescent's effort to reconcile perceived discrepencies between his own internal values and those of society. As a person is developing his own moral value system, he will experience a particular commitment to that system. If this system of values is obviously at variance with those of other significant groups, there will be an experience of dissonance. If the adolescent feels discomfort due to this dis-equilibrium in values, he/she (according to the cognitive development theorists will strive to relieve the internal pressure by conforming to the values of the group. Again, if the group values getting high on drugs, the vunerable child will tend to reconcile the dissonance by joining in with the peer group and get high also.

An adolescent, like an adult, will push toward congruence between his values and those of the greater society. Most adolescents have difficulty in tolerating dissonance in their value system, particularly if theirs does not match those of the peer group. This characteristic lends vunerability to the adolescent value system. If the young person is already suffering intense conflicts with identity and self confidence, then he is all the more vulnerable to adopting potentially self-destructive values (i.e., drug abuse, delinquent behavior, etc. It seems that the Identity Diffusions and Moratoriums are more prone to alter their values in a careless and impulsive manner. The Identity Achievements and Foreclosures tend to be more thoughtful and loyal to their value systems. The Foreclosures are particularly less likely to change their values if it would be contrary to what their parents would sanction. The Identity Achievements tend to experience more self confidence in their own integrity and decision making, and as a result, are more likely to change values in a thoughtful and careful manner.

An Ego To Be Reckoned With

In the first half of this century, the work of Sigmund Frued and other psychoanalysts served well to divert our understanding of adolescent ego development. Prior to 1960, it was generally held that early adolescence was a period full of dangerous oedipal sexual desires, and tremendous internal pressure to deal with these new and strong sexual conflicts. Much of adolescent behavior was defined in terms of sexual urges. This, unfortunately, drew a very skewed and distorted picture of the adolescent ego.

These beliefs led to the development of the "turmoil theory" of adolescent development. This theory held that adolescence was a hopelessly pre-psychotic stage that most children fortunately outgrew. Also, the theory proposed that the adolescent was subject to ego weakness; turbulence, maladjustment and psychotic-like states were normal (and even necessary) aspects of adolescent development.

This turmoil theory misled an entire generation of adolescent researchers. However, in the more recent past, new data has emerged which suggests that psychopathology in adolescents is not a normal part of the development sequence, and that disturbances and symptoms, if they exist, are not outgrown (Masterson, 1967, 1968). The work of Adelson (1966) and Offers (1963, 1975) strongly suggests that most adolescents do not experience serious turmoil, ego weakness, or sexual desires for their parents. The work of

Erickson helped to redirect our thinking away from the "turmoil" notion, and towards a belief that one of the basic tasks of adolescence is to establish autonomy. This has led to a commonly held belief that the ego is an organizational ego, one that has as its main task the fitting together of internal and external experience. Long term studies of psychotic patients have revealed that those individuals who exhibited psychotic behavior as adolescents, generally continued to do so long into adult life. One does not tend to outgrow a psychoses; treatment is generally required.

Josselson (1980) has synthesized some of Erickson's major concepts on ego development into what might be called a theory of integration:

1. Adolescence is intimately linked to the rest of the life cycle, with its own special tasks that have been in preparation all along — the notion of ego continuity.

2. Adolescence is a psychosocial demand that will be imposed on the individual, whether or not there is an internal push for it — a notion of adolescence as a maturational necessity.

3. Ego integration at adolescence is an emergent phenomenon, in the sense that the organization of aspects of self is more than the sum of the parts, and resides precisely in the manner in which the parts are synthesized — the notion of ego identity.

Researchers who investigate normal adolescents continue to find that development during adolescence is slow, gradual and unremarkable. Maturation in adolscence often takes place in steady, silent and nontumultuous ways. As mentioned earlier in the chapter, many have been guilty of attributing negative and harmful interpretations to behavior they determined unacceptable. Often, too much meaning is assigned to fairly unremarkable adolescent behavior. Understanding what is taking place within the adolescent can help us to separate the meaningful from the unmeaningful.

As the individual internalizes what was previously external, he also gains autonomy from it at the same time. At first, the young child is consoled by his parents when injured, insulted, or saddened by some event. Eventually, the child learns to console himself in the same way the parents did. As an adolescent, he can begin to take over this job and console himself much as his parents did and, as a result, gain independence from them. At first, the mother is introjected by the child — she is swallowed whole (Josselson, 1980). This process leads the adolescent to yet another crucial developmental turning point. The young person must learn to distinguish between his own ego experience and that of his introjected (internalized) parents and his own identifications. This process of individuation occurs over time and assists the adolescent to further crystalize his own unique ego self.

The adolescent task of individuation, then, is to gain difference and distance from the internalized parents, to transcend the infantile objectives. The experience of individuation is that of a sharpened sense of one's distinctiveness from others, a heightening of boundaries, and a feeling of selfhood and will. Blos (1967) puts it, "Individuation implies that the growing person takes increasing responsibility for what he does and what he is, rather that depositing this responsibility on the shoulders of those whose influence and tutelage he has grown up under (p. 168)."

When considering the process of individuation, there is a tendency to expect that the adolescent must overturn all the parental values and introjects. Yet, the young person can be quite successful at individuation, and still maintain much of the parental beliefs. The essential issue is that the individual adequately sift through for himself previous and current experience, to arrive at a new organizational ego. Opposition is only important in that it helps to make clear, to the self and others, that one is becoming autonomous and not surrendering.

At 15 John was eager to be grown up and be free of his parent's influence. He purposefully selected values contrary to what his parents believed. John felt it was important to be an independent thinker. As he grew older, he began to notice how similar his values were becoming to those originally held by his parents. Unknowingly, John had picked up many of his parent's values again — the same values he had originally rejected.

The adolescent appears to be dealing with two "parent identities," the reality parents and the introjected parents (the internalized image of mom and dad). In order to deal more effectively with the introjected parents, the young person may project onto the reality parents qualities which are not always accurate. For example, consider the adolescent who reacts harshly to the simple question, "Where are you going?" For the moment, the adolescent experiences the parent as controlling and denying autonomy. So, in an effort to perceive himself as an individual, he must "teach" the internal parent that he deserves to be treated as an adult. It is generally at this point when the parents retort with, "I'll treat you like an adult when you start acting like one." The adolescent already feels he is acting like an adult, and so the struggle goes on.

Adolescent attitudes about curfew are often at variance with those of the parents. The parents will firmly assert that 12 midnight is the absolute latest the child may stay out. However, the adolescent, through his perceived ability to think for himself, may decide that 1 a.m. is right for him. And so, when he arrives home at 1 instead of 12, he feels perfectly justified and prepared to suffer the "hassle" he will get from his parents. This type of autonomy struggle is generically different from that which occurs when the drug-abusing adolescent drags in three hours late. The conflict which ensues from the action has more to do with protecting one's continued use of drugs, than it does with true autonomy.

Prior to puberty, children tend to trust their parent's judgment above their own. They may break the rules, but they do not challenge the rightness of the rules. Children believe in the omnipotence of mom and dad. The child, in a sense, adopts the parent's ego as his own, and identifies himself through it. It is precisely this harmony that is shattered by the onset of puberty. New, exciting, and frightening feelings begin to emerge that can only be shared with peers in any meaningful way. Secrets about one's own body, and views about the opposite sex, suddenly become taboo to parents. Only the peer group is privileged to this information. All of a sudden, some things become too personal to share with those people with whom you have spent your whole life.

The early adolescent, ages 11 to 13, delights in his new feeling of separateness and autonomy, and often wants to act as though he had no parents at all. The adolescent defines himself primarily through saying "no" to the parents, or anyone else who tries to infringe upon his freedom. In some ways, this stage is like a second stage of omnipotence, as we would expect to find in the three-year-old. A young person of this age feels he can do anything — the self is all good; bad self representations are projected onto others (Josselson, 1980). At times, but not always, the adolescent will attempt to separate himself as a distinct person by finding ways to irritate his parents. This becomes another way of flexing his new-found will, and separating one's self from their parents in a more lasting way. The three-year-old is only testing his will, as he would play with a new toy to see how it works, and where the limits are. The three-year-old has no real need to permanently pull away from mom and dad.

Sometime after the adolescent has established some actual auto-nomy from the parents, he suddenly fully realizes he is functioning outside of parental scrutiny. The adolescent may then become anxious, and wish to restore harmony with the parents. One of the most common complaints to be heard from an adolescent is, "My parents don't understand me." This plea combines both their desire for distinctiveness and the wish for approval. If, in fact, the parents do not understand the adolescent, this confirms that he truly is an independent and separate individual. But, if the parents do not understand the adolescent, then this also may mean that they do not love him. As in early childhood, the adolescent still wants his parents at home if he needs them; otherwise, he would generally prefer that they stay out of his life. Still a rather tentative autonomy. This ambivalence over autonomy often leads to much of the pain experienced between parents and teenagers.

As the adolescent ego struggles to physically and emotionally separate from the parents, we sometimes find that this does not necessarily imply intrapsychic individuation. Adolescents who feel incompetent at successfully individuating themselves may exhibit wholesale abrogation of the parents, through excessive attempts to physically withdraw. These adolescents demand inordinate amounts of time away from the home, and react intensely to any effort to control their coming and going. They act as though "getting away" from their parents will get them away from their troublesome introjects, and such dramatic disengagement efforts seldom serve to speed up the process. Young people who abuse drugs may believe this is assisting in their separating from their parents. Unfortunately, this assumption can lead to disaster.

The separation and individuation processes do not always keep pace with each other. At times, the adolescent's drive for separateness exceeds his abilities to function autonomously, and he may well have to make decisions without the ego resources to do so. This will subject the adolescent to repeated painful experiences, and that most dreaded feeling of all, humiliation! This is when the young person must humble himself and admit a need for parental support. Yet, this request for help goes against the adolescent's need to appear autonomous. When adolescents are interviewed privately, they frequently will admit to an appreciation for parental support, rules, standards and limits.

Advancement in cognitive development also contributes to the growth of the ego. As the young person learns how to construct hypothesis about how the world works, he/she also discovers some limitations to the parent's ego. When an adolescent tells us that his parents do not understand the world as he finds it, he is often, in fact, accurate. The "generation gap" is due, in part, to differences in the life histories of the two age groups. The world has changed, and the adolescent is likely to be more accepting of the current status than his parents.

When looking at ego development in relation to the peer group, we find an interesting process occurring. In early and middle adolescence, we find the peer group is of utmost importance, and the person does all he or she can to effectively align him/herself with the group. Later, the young person has to again re-experience the individuation process, but this time it involves separating from the peers. It is quite amazing how coersive adolescents can be with each other, and actually tolerate it. Peers at first serve to mitigate the pull toward the parents, supporting the individuation aspects of the ego. "Do you think I did the right thing?" Adolescents are forever asking each other this question in one form or another. And because adolescents have not yet mastered adult diplomacy, the answer is invariably "yes." Adolescents find it difficult to tolerate differentness from those on whom they rely for ego support.

Since the adolescent is rejecting the efforts of the parents to support and direct him, he then creates a need to regain that support through his peers. The adolescent hungers for group participation, and this provides a defensive function in warding off the experience of inner emptiness. There is safety in numbers. This period of ego development can be intensely lonely and fearful. The adolescent both enjoys and is frightened by his new autonomy. And so the compulsion to be with friends actually becomes an adaptive function, and provides new ego-sharing experiences and new identifications.

It cannot be overstated how important ego development can be to the adolescent. In earlier childhood years, the individual modulates his behavior, based upon internal parental introjects. If the children grow up in an environment where they are validated and supported, they tend to develop good psychosocial skills. The intensely insecure child, with poor psychosocial skills, is not well for prepared the pressures of adolescence. This period demands disengagement from the parents. If the child is unable to do so, then he may collapse back into the parent's influence and control. This is essentially an unhealthy position for the adolescent. This child never seems to get started with adolescence, and remains in an ongoing internal struggle with insecurity about moving away from the parents. The egos of these children can be characterized by passivity and an avoidance of goal setting (Identity Diffusion).

Another possible phenomenon can be the prolonging of adolescence beyond its normal point of closure. Overly protective parents can contribute to this. These are parents who, for whatever reason, need the child to remain at home (more on this in the next chapter). The period of crisis and limit-testing is kept open indefinitely, as the adolescent strives to avoid the finality of choices. In these young people, narcissitic aggrandizement is expressed in their sense of potential (fantasy), but never seems to develop into real independent action.

Along about middle adolescence, the young person may realize, with a sense of shock, that he, in fact, cannot invent himself as he would like. He finds himself stuck with certain traits which he is powerless to change. The unhappy and shy adolescent may decide to become like her more outgoing friends as a way to escape her shyness. Yet, the basic tendency to be shy remains, and she is infuriated when a friend accuses her of being shy. "How can I be shy, since I have worked so hard not to be?" The shock of our powerlessness to alter our selves can be devastating.

Adolescents tend to have peers they "love" and peers they "hate." Often these are the same people, even on the same day. A friend can move from best friend to worst enemy in a matter of hours. Eventually, the adolescent becomes more comfortable with ambivalence toward a friend, and can recognize both negative and positive qualities. This is an essential developmental step away from childhood totalism, and toward a more balanced view of the world. Friends can possess both qualities we like and qualities we dislike, and still be counted as friends.

Much of the preadolescent behavior can be predictors of adult adjustment (Peskin & Livson, 1972). Preadolescents whose behavior indicated independence, self-confidence and intellectual curiosity, were most likely to grow into well integrated adults (i.e. Identity Achievements). It seems that movement from relative preadolescent stability to *mild* emotional disruption in adolescence is found to produce the most favorable adult outcome. A period of mild unrest in early adolescence has been found to be associated with psychosocial maturity in later stages of adolescence and adulthood.

Throughout this chapter, there has been reference to early, middle, and late adolescence. It would be understandable to expect that movement from one stage of adolescence to another would tend to follow a chronological sequence. Yet, this is not always the case. One stage is not always clearly distinguishable from another. Also, there may be overlapping between stages. The following is an effort to clearly define these three stages, yet the reader is cautioned to remember that a given 16-year-old could well be in any one of these.

> *Early adolescence* can be characterized by intense conflicts with earlier stages of development. Previously-held beliefs are questioned and tested for validity. The young person is quite enamored with his/her new intellect, and tends to overestimate his/her abilities. Primarily, the adolescent is caught up in an effort to reject the parental introjects and establish his/her own capabilities.

Middle adolescence has to do with the shift in cognitive capacity to formal operations, which aids the ego in its attempt to be realistic, rather than dominated by feelings of guilt and blame. This increased cognitive ability allows the middle adolescent more self-consciousness; the adolescent can now take the self as an object of reflective thought. This awareness of self allows for the gradual replacement of group values with self-determined standards. A failure in ego delvopment at this point may precipitate movement backward into an earlier stage of development.

Late adolescence is marked by the theme of consolidation. The ego vacillation of middle adloscence gives way to more confident, predictable, and reliable ego functioning. Emotional outbursts have been mastered, and emotions are both tolerated and found to be enriching. Internal conflicts are less threatening, and the person is more secure in his/her ability to test reality and reach his/her own solutions.

Again, movement from one stage to another may be done in a halting and jerking fashion. The early adolescent may, at times, return to the concrete operations phase, and so some understanding of this is necessary. Elkind (1967) offers some useful criteria for this stage. The major cognitive task of a child in this stage is the mastering of classes, relations, and quantities. The child also rises to a new level of egocentrism. The preadolescent has the rudiments of formal operations, and can begin to grasp simple hypotheses and use them to explain a set of facts and beliefs about particular phenomenon in the world. The concrete child begins to perceive this new ability in an arrogant way, and may look down on those believed to be "simple-minded." When a child in this stage constructs a hypothesis, or formulates a strategy, he assumes that the product is imposed by the facts (there is no other possible conclusion), rather than from his own mental activity (personal interpretation). Consider the child who has memorized every one of her favorite TV programs and its respective channels. Then the child and her family travel to another city and check into a hotel. The child turns on the TV and is shocked to find strange programs on the channel that always before carried her favorite program. The child then enters into a stubborn debate with her parents about something being wrong with the TV. The father says to his pouting daughter, "Honey, in this town they must have different channels than we have back home, and maybe the programs come on at different times, too." "You're wrong Dad. I know when every program comes on, and on which channel. This set must be broken, call the manager," insists the daughter. This child cannot reconcile that the facts are contrary to her beliefs. She had such complete confidence in her grasp of a segment of life that she cannot conceive of another possibility. When her position is challenged, she does change her stance, but only reinterprets the data to fit with her original assumption. "Well I know I'm right, but the hotel must have switched the channels on this TV, and now channel 3 is really channel 12. I don't know why they would do such a stupid thing."

The phenomenon discussed above lends support to the common belief that children 12 and under are not good canididates for impatient treatment. The intensity of the environment and the rational confrontations presented there are more than the preadolescent can cope with. The complex concepts presented in impatient treatment require advanced cognitive abilities beyond the concrete operation stage. Preadolescents may eventually comply with treatment "dogma," but rarely internalize it.

A few more thoughts on egocentrism would be helpful here. The adolescent who now can realize his ability to think independently, and create new thoughts, can become completely caught up in this process. Egocentrism emerges as an inability to differentiate between the focus of other's thoughts and the focus of one's own thoughts. Since he fails to differentiate between what others are thinking and his own preoccupations, he assumes that other people are as admiring, or as critical of him as he is of himself. It is this belief that others are preoccupied with his appearance and behavior that constitutes the egocentrism of the adolescent (Elkind, 1967).

While watching adolescents in groups, we may have noticed that each of them is concerned with being observed, than with being the observer. Each young person is simultaneously an actor to himself, and an audience to others. So, adolescents spend a great deal of time rehearsing for the next real, or imagined, social encounter. The adults who happen to observe this phenomenon can find it difficult to tolerate, since so much importance is placed upon what seems to be superficial values.

According to Elkind, adolescent egocentrism is thus overcome by a two-fold transformation. On the cognitive plane, it is overcome by the gradual differentiation between one's own preoccupations and the thoughts of others; while on the affective plane, it is overcome by a gradual integration of the feelings of others, with one's own emotions.

The adolescent ego is both a thing to be reckoned with and respected. There are essential operations occurring during ego development, and this will, to a great extent, determine identity and security for the emerging adult personality.

Theories of Development

This section is not intended to be an exhaustive survey of developmental theories, but a brief outline of some basic concepts associated with the more popular theories. Some of what will be presented here does not technically fall within the category of "theory," but represents some significant work done in the field which has had a strong influence upon our thinking about adolescence. As stated earlier, much of this chapter has been devoted to describing the "normal" adolescent, and the same will be true of this section.

The work of people like Piaget and Erickson was organized around an effort to try to understand some predictable and sequential stages of child, adolescent and adult development. When Erickson first began writing about develpment, he constructed a sequential series of stages of growth which he called the "theory of socialization" (Erickson, 1963). Erickson was most concerned with how we socialize with each other, and how our children are prepared for adulthood. Erickson divided this process of socialization into eight stages. The stages of development are not necessarily exclusive of each other, and it is expected there would be overlap as one moves through them. Erickson's stages are as follows:

1. Trust vs Mistrust

2. Autonomy vs Shame

3. Initiative vs Guilt

4. Industry vs Inferiority

5. Identity vs Identity Diffusion

6. Intimacy vs Isolation

7. Generativity vs Self Absorption

8. Integrity vs Despair

The first three stages are concerned with early and middle childhood development. The stages have to do with tasks that need to be completed before the individual can move on to the next stage. So, the young child is about the task of learning to trust others in the world, seeking out his/her own autonomy and ability to function alone at times, and finally, learning about taking care of specific tasks on his own, without parental coercion. The end of childhood and the beginning of adolescence is marked by the task of learning how to "work," using related skills, and gaining a sense of accomplishment.

The period known as adolescence is most clearly marked by the struggle between identity and identity diffusion. The adolescent's task is to find a way of separating from the parent figures, thereby creating his/her own self image. The end of adolescence is marked by a new task which has to do with giving up some of the recently-gained autonomy, in order to have intimate relationships with others. This can be a particularly difficult stage if there have been problems in the previous stages. If the young person has not been successful in gaining autonomy, then he may have considerable trouble allowing himself to be intimate with others. The adolescent may still be too protective of his fragile identity.

The adult, according to Erickson, is about the task of caregiving for others, and is less concerned with his own personal interests (preparation for raising children). However, childrearing is not the only way an adult can care for others. Finally, as the end of adult life draws near, the issue of integrity becomes more important. The individual begins to evaulate his worth as a person. "Have I accomplished what I wanted, or has my life been misspent?"

Logan, in his article on re-conceptualizing Erickson's identity stage (1983), believes that our youth are less concerned with developing work skills than they used to be. We, as a culture, are becoming more concerned with our existential life identity than our instrumental identity. "Be yourself" is now the byword, instead of the old "make something of yourself." We seem less concerned with becoming builders and makers, and are more oriented towards being receivers of the experiences of the world. In a sense, we are becoming a society of consumers rather than producers. Children have fewer opportunities to actually accomplish something tangible, but instead are only offered experiences. The future is running headlong at us and we find ourselves having less control over it. As Toffler described in his book, *The Third Wave* (1980), we no longer feel like we are the cause of the future, but we are more a result of it.

These ideas seem to have profound implications for adolescents, in that they are in the midst of a cultural phenomenon, as well as directly affected by it. A new sense of narcissism is sweeping the land. Young people are offered fewer opportunities to develop instrumental values based upon what they can accomplish. Identity is based upon one's own experience of the self. This gives us few external ques to use to assess how well we are doing. These significant changes have occurred since Erickson first developed his theory of socialization.

Piaget's theory is one of cognitive development. It is concerned with the changes in how we think as we age. Piaget (1950) believed that thought was actually internalized action. Piaget views development in four "operational stages," or levels of thinking. Piaget's stages are as follows:

1. Sensori-Motor Operations

2. Concrete Operations

3. Pre-operations

4. Formal Operations

The sensori-motor operations are those operations carried out in action, and there is very little thought involved — at least as most of us would define thought, such as bringing food from a plate to one's mouth. Concrete operations are internal actions which can be reversed, but they involve actual behavior (i.e., putting together a puzzle). Pre-operations deal with the internalization process of thinking, and tend to be rigid rather than flexible, such as the example cited earlier, where the daughter insisted she knew which programs were on chich channels. Formal operations are not resticted to actual transformations of reality; they deal with abstractions and creative thoughts which are independent of reality, such as the idea, "What if the atom bomb had not been dropped on Hiroshima?"

Formal operational thinking emerges during the adolescent period. The formal thinker conducts "though experiments" prior to acting, and consequently proceeds in a systematic, rather than a trial-and-error manner when solving problems (Berzonsky, 1978). Recent research suggests that all adolescents, and even adults, do not necessarily develop complete formal reasoning powers. Furthermore, those adolescents who do reason formally do not do so in an all-pervasive manner; they may reason formally in some situations, but not in others. The adolescent can frequently be plagued by a constant vacillation between formal operations and earlier levels of reasoning, for example, the adolescent who can intellectually disdain any use for drugs, but when tempted by peers, may spontaneously develop a new and contradictory viewpoint.

The concrete reasoner does reason via internalized action, but centers such actions on real manipulations of the world; reality is the only possibility. This young person finds it difficult to deal effectively with hypothetical statements that are in conflict with concrete reality. The formal reasoner, when confronted with a problem, envisions possible causes and combinations of causes, and then proceeds to act in a systematic manner.

This formal reasoning ability seems to work well for the adolescent, until he has to apply it to himself. The egocentrism of the adolescent may make it difficult for him to "intellectualize," or think formally, about problems relevant to himself. It is not uncommon for the adolescent to regress back to concrete operations when trying to rationalize his own behavior. This can be true of adults as well.

Berzonsky (1978) contends that cognitive development as conceived by Piaget is in need of some expansion. Berzonsky does not vision crisp demarcations between Piaget's stages, and so offers the Branch Model. The Branch Model follows Piaget's through concrete operations, and then divides formal operations into aesthetic knowledge and personal knowledge. Both classes of knowledge are then subject to four more categories: behavior content; symbolic content; semantic content; and, figural content. Aesthetic knowledge involves the type of knowing that is experienced directly while personal knowledge is more existential in nature.

When considering the elements of the "Drive Theory," we look at adolescence as a period of development where the person is driven to accomplish certain experiences. These experiences could be better described as changes in self, and so the adolescent is driven to change in the following ways:

1. a new drive towards sex

2. change in social expectations

3. changes in self concept

4. a need to find one's own identity

The Drive Theory differs from Erickson's stages in that he believed the stages were linked together, and predetermined each other (task accomplishment). The Drive Theory proposes a class of experiences which is common to all adolescents. These classes are not particularly linked together, but are autonomous from each other. This theory haunts back to the psycholanalytic notion that all development is predicated upon sexual development, and that we are driven by deep forces to do what we do.

The California Growth Studies of Jones and Baley (1950) related development to physical characteristics rather than intellec-

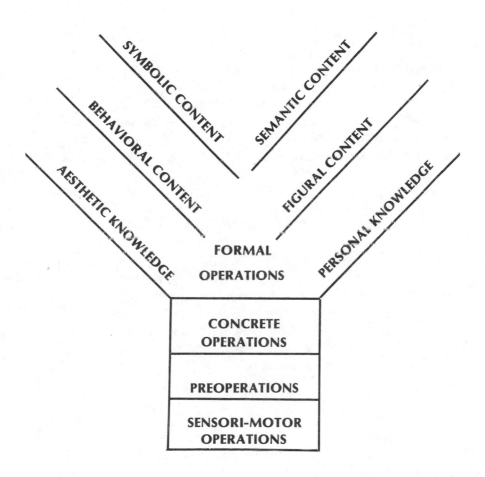

BRANCH MODEL OF

COGNITIVE DEVELOPMENT

tual/ego tasks. Jones and Baley studied adolescent body types and the rate of development, and found some correlation between temperament, abilities, and physical development. They found that boys who developed early experienced many more advantages than the late-maturing boys. The early maturing boys found life easier, and were more confident in themselves. The late maturing boys had more trouble with physical and social experiences, and possessed less self confidence. However, the early maturers experienced difficulty with intimate relationships in adult life, partly because their egos were so strong, that it was difficult for them to allow themselves to be vulnerable. And, also, because they had previously relied upon their physcial prowess to see them through. The late maturing boys were more successful in adult intimate relationships, in part because they had to work harder to make friends when they were younger.

Jones and Baley found that early maturing girls were at a disadvantage, because they tended to rush themselves into experiences for which they were not really ready. These girls tended to have more social problems than the late maturing girls in the long run. The late maturing girls had to learn self esteem, and the others seemed to have had it handed to them, due to their attractiveness and/or sexual development. It would tend to follow, then, that the early maturing girls would also be more at-risk to develop problems with drug abuse. These girls will tend to overestimate their abilities. These findings seem to be relevant to our culture, and not necessarily to others.

The study of Jones and Baley may place too much importance upon physical growth characteristics, yet there does seem to be some validity to the idea of advantages and disadvantages related to rates of maturation. This data, along with many other issues raised above, must be taken into consideration when assessing the development of an adolescent. As is true when assessing any human condition, it is essential to look at all of the variables which may have any bearing upon the final conclusions. Having a theoretical frame of reference is also important, and it is not suggested that one limit oneself to only one set of ideas. Many of the theories presented in this chapter have valid components and can prove to be useful in understanding the adolescent.

Adolescence In Perspective

It is no longer appropriate to refer to adolescence as that perplexing "state" between childhood and adulthood. As Erickson, Piaget and other have revealed, adolescence is a period of life with a definite and intentional purpose. Futhermore, it no longer makes sense to categorize the adolescent as "in a temporary state of maladaptation." The adolescent is adapting, and in a quite normal fashion, considering the task before him. Again, determining the normal from the abnormal can be a delicate and subtle distinction. John Meeks (1973) offers the following cautions:

> Adolescence is a fluid state;
>
> It is necessary to have a distinction between disturbed behavior, which is an exaggeration of common problems, and real pathology;
>
> Too often moral value judgments can enter into diagnosing;
>
> In a rapidly-changing society, it becomes more and more difficult to differentiate "sick" behavior from behavior that is appropriately extreme, in the face of real and serious external problems.

This time of adolescence is a time for consolidation of physical, social and emotional resources, towards the development of a complete person ready to face the world independently. An independent self-indentity must be determined from a prior parent-determined identity. This task requires the young person to establish a sense of mutuality, unity and continuity (Handel, 1980). Mutuality arises from the adolescent's awareness that his own self-perceptions are congruent with the way significant others perceive him. Unity comes from a sense of wholeness and harmony among the different selves making up the identity. And, continuity comes from an ability to hold a view of present, past and future selves.

As was mentioned at the beginning of this chapter, it is essential, when working with adolescents, to keep in perspective their unique task, our biases, and the context of their behavior. If we were to isolate one developmental characteristic and only study it in isolation, it may, in fact, appear to be abnormal and radical. One piece of adolescent behavior by itself may mean nothing and appear maladaptive. But when we consider the numerous complicated tasks, and all of adolescence to be task-oriented, then the behavior may seem less troublesome. Before moving on to the study of the chemically dependent adolescent, we must first pause to put in perspective what this thing called adolescence is! Our frame of reference will be critical to the later assessment and treatment of the dependent young person.

Chapter 2

Social and Family Relationships

When parents are interviewed about why they believe their adolescent became involved with drugs, they invariably say something like, "Our son wouldn't do something like that on his own. It was those friends he hung around with." It is sentiments like these that lead many parents to believe they are at war with their own neighborhood. "We raise our children to be good kids, and now all that is going down the drain because of some punk down the street." The outside world can become a very threatening place to the stability of a family, yet children cannot be successfully protected from it.

Peer relationships are essential to the process of individuation for the adolescent desiring to pull away from his parents. However, even parents who appreciate this process can be appalled by the power and seemingly negative influence of their children's friends. "It seems like Jennifer is never at home, and when she is, she is talking to one of her friends on the phone." To be obsessed with one's friends is not abnormal for the young person. This is characteristic of both the non-dependent child, and the chemically dependent one. Excessive dependence upon peers is not a characteristic of drug abuse, or chemical dependency. What goes on within those relationships and how they are used is of some concern, and demands careful attention. The uninvolved parent who allows his/her teenagers to do what they wish, with whom they wish, without any supervision, is making a careless mistake. Also, the uninvolved parent is generally the creator of an insecure and vulnerable child.

If we recall the four identity types of chapter one, we remember that the Identity Diffusion and Moratoriums were the most vulnerable to drug abuse. These individuals are also more prone to select unhealthy and disruptive peer relationships. It should be mentioned here that no social position, or family environment, can completely protect an adolescent from chemical dependency. Even the "best" family can be vulnerable to this problem. Simply identifying a set of criteria does not ensure accurate predictions of future dependency problems. A broad understanding of adolescents is necessary to effectively treat this population.

Peers, Friend or Foe

What is the purpose, or function, for peer relationships? As mentioned in Chapter One, the peer relationship becomes a vehicle to propel the adolescent into a state of perceived independence from his parents. The process of individuation is a major task, and would be very difficult to accomplish alone.

The aloof and isolated adolescent can experience great difficulty in achieving independence from mom and dad. This person may seem self-sufficient and mature, and generally excels in academic pursuits. It is this author's belief that this psuedo-independent person's development is incomplete, due to his lack of involvement with peers. The isolated child may reliably please mom and dad, and seem to be responsible and independent. But there is false security in this type of profile. The child is overly dependent upon his parent's approval, and has not really individuated himself, nor established a true sense of "self."

Of course, the adolescent who places all of his energy into achieving his friend's approval is no more independent than the one described above. However, it is believed that this is a temporary state, with true independence to follow, as the individual begins to reject some of the peer values later in adolescence. To begin this process, the adolescent must first use the peer group to pull away from the influence of the parents. Once this is accomplished, then the child can begin to sort out what he truly believes and values.

Another purpose of peer relationships is to provide the adolescent someone with whom to be intimate. There are new thoughts, feelings and experiences which the young person wishes to keep from his/her parents. Also, the peer provides a sounding board with whom to check things out. It is important to secure the approval of someone else when struggling with your own inner feelings. To know that your friends feel the same way as you makes you feel more secure. But, if a friend does not agree, then the adolescent feels betrayed and may seek out a new friend in whom to confide. This, in part, is why adolescent relationships are so prone to frequent changes. The young adolescent is unable to tolerate disagreement with his ideas, and will seek someone who will agree. On the other hand, relationships can form between adolescents which can last for a lifetime. That special friend with whom you can always share your most intimate secrets is a valuable "possession."

Because adolescents can be so insecure in their own sense of self, they are reluctant to violate a friendship. They are loath to "squeal" on each other. Even if I disagree with your beliefs and behavior, I am inclined to go along with you just so I do not lose your friendship. And so adolescents can easily become co-conspirators in a variety of schemes and secrets. If my friend confides in me about her drug use and wants to "turn me on" also, I'm caught in an ethical dilemma. Even if I am able to turn her down, I am still obliged to keep the secret. Once I have agreed to keep the secret, then I am caught in the "trick bag." I must be ever careful of my parents, because I know they are always trying to catch me at something anyway. As a result, kids become defensive with their parents even when it is not really necessary. The adolescent may perceive that mom and dad are trying to get something out of them, when all they really care about is, "What time will you be home tonight?"

Parents can possess some interesting views of peers. The knowledgeable and involved parents will generally see their child's friend as a necessary support system. Due to this realization, healthy parents will attempt to support their child's friends and be tolerant of problems. It is the wise parent who is careful to not speak critically of his/her children'a friends.

It is common for parents to view their children's friends as adversaries with whom they must compete. Some parents are jealous and resentful of the time and energy given to peer relationships, and the pitiful miniscule amount devoted to the family by their child. This attitude can create serious problems in a family when one, or both, parents tend to constantly berate their children's friends. However, adolescents can align themselves with rather unsavory characters who can lead them into trouble. As will be discussed in a later chapter, an abrupt change in your children's friends can be an indicator of a problem. The drug-abusing adolescent will tend to associate with other using kids to seek support for his/her behavioral changes. The heretofore friendless child may discover an automatic circle of "friends" when beginning to use drugs. If you have perceived yourself as friendless, you are not likely to be too fussy if your new friends tend to be on the "scruffy" side. At least, you now have someone to associate with.

Parents of normal adolescents will discover that peers can begin to undermine many of the values they have previously instilled in their children. When adolescents are presented with new attitudes and behaviors, they may temporarily reject what they previously did not even question. Parents are advised to view this erosion of values as transitory, and not assume that they have failed at their job. The questioning process is necessary, and the healthy family will survive this period with minimal discomfort if they are patient.

Parents who offer frequent verbal resistance to their child's attempts at independence are only asking for misery. The more parents complain about the peer relationships, the more they reinforce the child to become more extreme. It is best to set reasonable and flexible guidelines, and let pass some of the less important issues (i.e., clean room, etc.).

Chemically Dependent Relationships

Chemically dependent kids tend toward peer relationships which serve somewhat different purposes than the normal population. These kids have few, if any, true friendships. Their relationships are characterized by mutual manipulation, extreme intensity, and are of short duration. These relationships are organized around one common bond, getting high. There is no other reason to get together unless it is to get high, or to procure drugs. There is generally little, or no emotional bonding. There are no shared interests, no shared feelings, no shared history. These kids know very little about each other. Friends are to be used to your own advantage — they have no other real purpose.

These adolescents may believe they have many close friends, but this is a drug-distorted perception. The effects of the drugs make them feel they have a special and intimate bond. But, there is no depth to this feeling, it only exists because a drug has created the feeling. The more children become involved with drugs, the less able they are to objectively evaluate anything, especially their friends. Because one's friends may supply the drugs, the adolescent will be bitterly defensive of them. This is not because he truly cares about them, but because he does not want to risk losing his source. This is why the drug-abusing adolescent will be so secretive about who his friends are. They fear that their parents are going to discover their use, and so are prepared to defend themselves at all times. They will react intensely to a sincere question like, "Who are you going to the movie with tonight?" The paranoid drug abuser suspects this is a manipulative question, intended to trip him up and force him to disclose his true intentions.

Another characteristic of depededent peer relationships is that these kids are non-evaluative of each other. The drugs can impose a false sense of omnipotence, and so whatever one wants to do must be all good. Also, these adolescents may feel they are the advanced and enlightened ones, and can do no wrong. This denial can become contagious so that the entire social group maintains a collective consciousness which no one dares violate for fear he/she will be rejected.

In many dependent adolescents, their defensive attitudes can be understood as intense guilt. The lifestyle of the drug-abusing adolescent is most obviously at variance to the values of his parents, and even his siblings. For the family to know the real extent of his involvement would be very painful for everyone. This experience can create tremendous internal stress for the average 15-year-old drug abuser. The only way the drug abusers possess to cope with this problem is to keep everyone they care about at arms length. The child who often expresses a desire to just get away for a while, may be saying that he cannot stand the pressure anymore. Any kind of proximity with his family simply increases the stress level, and the guilt level.

Family Interactions

The healthy family is characterized by mutually reciprocal and, as such, supportive roles. The healthy family has its problems, but interacts in a way which is oriented towards the solving of problems in a supportive manner. All families are protective in nature. Families will protect each other from pain, discomfort, outside threats, and sometimes, even from the truth.

At the head of the healthy family resides the competent parents, or parent. When two parents reside in the family, and the household flows harmoniously then a fundamentally cooperative attitude must exist. Effective parents support each other, never undermine each other, and are consistent in their disciplinary efforts. This, of course, sounds idealistic, and it is, but parents who realize the value of cooperative efforts, and strive to practice this are generally more effective. These parents realize that at times their children are going to try and divide them. It takes a strong commitment as parents to stand together on most issues, even when one may disagree with another's decision.

Healthy families are also tolerant of each other's failures, and do not expect perfection from the members. The parents of these families realize the awkward struggles of their teenage children are natural and temporary. They understand their children's need to become independent, and that the ego develops in spurts, not all at once. Mature and responsible behavior one day may be followed the next by infantile outbursts or tantrums. Stamina and objectivity are necessary for the healthy parent.

Generally, the democratic parent can best pull off the attitudes described above. However, the benevolent dictator, who can intuitively envision his child's needs can be equally as effective. Regardless of the parent's style, it requires a careful balance between supervision and independence to raise a healthy and competent child. Knowing when to restrict and when to let go is the key to success. The healthy parent is continually striving to be consistent in his activities, but also adjusting the rules according to the capabilities of the child.

In the author's practice, experience has shown that healthy families possess clearly defined problem-solving procedures. Maybe all problems are solved through the family meeting. Or, the parents get together, alone, to discuss an issue and then announce the solution together to the rest of the family. The procedure is less important than the fact that the parents set the example and consistently follow it as a team.

Finally, healthy families tend to possess a sense of history. There is a clear transmission of family values from one generation to another. This helps the family members to better understand who they are and where they came from. The extended family is respected, and ongoing contact is maintained over time.

As mentioned before, even the healthiest of families can produce a chemically dependent child. The following section will describe the common characteristics of a family system where one, or more dependent members may live.

Chemically Dependent Family Interactions

Imagine an armada of seventeenth century sailing ships making their way across stormy seas, and the decks are constantly rolling and pitching. Then focus your attention upon one individual ship where there is a loose cannon careening back and forth across the deck as the crew jump and run trying to avoid being hit by the runaway cannon. This scene is not unlike life in a family where there is a chemically dependent member who is actively using drugs, or alcohol. The dependent member is a threat to the safety and welfare of the rest of the family. Everyone must learn how to avoid being run over; occasionally, individuals are not quick enough to get out of the way. But, over time, most members of the family learn to stay out of the way of the cannon, and adapt to its presence. Some members stay below decks to avoid the problem, and are never seen. And, others to climb the masts and make a lot of noise, trying to point out those below the threat of the loose cannon.

In the chemically dependent family system, there exists an ongoing struggle for power and control. The alcoholic parent, or the drug abusing adolescent can wield a great deal of power, even when absent from the home. Family members alter their interactions in response to the dependent member's incompetence, and try to compensate for strife created in the family. The family attemps to protect, appease, ignore, dominate and buy off the dependent person, just to return to a homeostatic balance.

Parents of chemically dependent children often find that they do not always agree on how to best handle this "loose cannon." One parent may be overly permissive, and the other too strict. Some parents can be characterized as fluctuating from overinvolvement to underinvolvement. Regardless of their style, parents who do not take a unified appoach to their problem child are going to sink the ship. This parental conflict creates an opportunity for the child to split the parents apart and neutralize them. This inconsistent parenting is characteristic of parents with chemically dependent children, yet perfectly understandable. Most loving parents want to give their child the benefit of the doubt, especially those who have over-identified with their child.

In some families where there is serious marital conflict, or one of the parents is alcoholic, scapegoating of the children may occur. It may be too threatening for the parents to interact directly about their problems, and so one or more of the children become a target for their anger. The scapegoated child may often turn out to be the one who later becomes chemically dependent. This may, in part, be due to a desire to achieve relief through drugs, as well as a misguided effort to save the family, but sacrifice one self.

In chemically dependent family systems, there is often a long history of alcoholism and drug addiction. The children may know this, then again have no knowledge of previous generations. The pattern of dependent interactions has been passed from one generation to the next, and becomes a familial heritage.

Step families are often fertile territory for drug-abusing adolescents to develop. If the child feels unaccepted by the step-parent, or ignored, or does not accept the new parent himself, then drug abuse can become an attractive outlet. Drug abuse can also become and effective means to draw attention to one self and away from the new parent.

Children from chemically dependent homes are often the victims of child-abuse — physical, verbal and sexual. This is a devastating experience for the children, and is something they feel they must keep to themselves and never tell anyone. Recent research has indicated that many anorexic girls and women were sexually abused by their fathers at an early age.

The same phenomenom seems to be happening with chemically dependent adolescents. Chemical dependency counselors have been reporting a high incidence of incest among their adolescent patients for several years now. Also, chemically dependent adolescents are often sexually promiscuous and are totally inept at forming healthy and appropriate heterosexual relationships. Obviously, a teenage girl who has been sexually molested by her father is going to be handicapped when it comes to relationships with other boys. Drugs become a convenient, and somewhat effective, means to turn off the guilt and shame experienced due to the incest. Furthermore, drugs may allow the girl to overcome her anxiety with boys and experience a sense of confidence. Unfortunately, drugs may cause the girl to relax too much. She is not in control, the drugs are.

This false sense of security and sensuality can lead drug dependent teenagers into a lifetime of relationship problems. These problems can persist, even after sobriety is achieved. These children still don't know how to relate to the opposite sex appropriately. The shadow of guilt still follows them, and they will need intensive therapy to overcome their sense of disgust for themselves as a sexual being.

Chemically dependent family systems are most generally experiencing what one could identify as an interactional disorder. The way this family interacts is impaired and does not resemble the healthier patterns described above. Whether the interactional disorder is in reponse to the dependent member, or the other way around, is a mute point. Chemically dependent families characteristically interact in an intensely protective, rigid, repetitive and denying manner. It matters little who begot the problem, only that they learn how to change their patterns of interaction. In this way, the dependent member can begin to get well, and the entire system can begin to function in the supportive manner necessary for positive growth.

Growing Up In The Drug Culture

Regardless of the statistics one reads, the drug problem in this country is not going away and is still a rampant epidemic. We have a cultural base of experience with drugs which is now in its third generation. "Stoned out hippies" from the sixties are now grandparents to adolescents who are just now beginning to experiment with drugs. There exists a broad foundation of drug experience within our culture. This experience has touched every American to some extent in the last 25 years. We cannot escape this phenomenon, and we most certainly cannot deny it. Our relationship with drugs is a dominant thread which weaves its way through the fabric of American life.

Flower Children and Cowboys

It is the author's belief that our nation's obsession with drugs grew out of a misguided notion about revolution, and an attraction to fantasy. In the '60s, many of our youth believed that a way to cause revolution was to begin with internal liberation of the spirit. The belief was that each person must liberate him/herself and then serve as an example to others. By freeing the human spirit, anything was then possible. In essence, these are the basic principles upon which our country was founded. The Constitution declares our right to pursue happiness. Some people sincerly believed that drug use was a valid way to accomplish their goal of liberation and revolution. Many of these folks adopted, or were assigned, the name "flower children."

Other members of our culture in the '60s and '70s were initially inspired by notions of liberation and revolution, but this later changed into another experience. Drugs opened up a brand new fantasy world for many. There was a strong movement among our youth to "get back to nature." People "dropped out" of the mainstream culture, and actually regressed back to an earlier culture. As one who lived in a commune for a while, the author can vividly remember acting out many childhood fantasies. There was a cowboy mentality sweeping the nation. Adolescents and young adults became fascinated with a style of dress and lifestyle that resembled pioneer days. Kids who had grown up in suburbia were heading for the wilderness, living in teepees, building log cabins, and learning to live off the land. Everyone wanted to be "natural." Drugs seemed to help to create and maintain this group fantasy. There was a belief in a spiritual relationship between doing "organic" drugs and living in simple harmony with the environment. Again, there was a combination of some admirable values and misguided means to those admirable ends.

During this period, our culture shifted into a casual attitude characterized by introspection and experimental permissiveness. "If it feels good, do it," became a frequently expressed value among young people. Personal adventure and rebellion were values encouraged by a large segment of the population. If one was not a part of the "counter culture," then one was an "imperialist pig." These ideas and values became deeply rooted in a segment of the population. Even today, those basic notions of revolution exist, but have become distorted and perverted.

Among some of today's youth, there exists a strong belief in serving the self, and that is a right we all possess. But there is nothing behind this value in terms of betterment of the culture as a whole.

One simply serves himself because it feels good. And again, drugs are helpful in making one feel good. Drugs intensify the senses and can make most any experience more enjoyable.

Fifty years ago, few Americans used drugs other thanan occasional aspirin. Drugs simply were not available to the average person. Also, there was a pervasive distrust of drugs, Today, the use of prescription drugs is widely accepted. The pharmeceutical companies constantly bombard us with the safe benefits of certain drugs. Also, drugs are available everywhere. One can purchase a wide array of over-the-counter drugs at the neighborhood convenience mart. Beer and wine commercials appear on television depicting an array of glamourous benefits from consuming these beverages.

In the past 30 years, there have been dramatic changes in our national attitude towards drug use, both legal and illegal. Like it or not, the phenomena of the last 30 years have filtered down through our society to its deepest levels.

Flower Children Grow Up

Those of us who participated in the counter culture movement, or received the label "flower children," are now parents ourselves. Although we may have at one time valued a permissive and liberated attitude, most adults can now see that "too much of a good thing" can be harmful. There are few adults today who believe that there is any redeeming value in drug experimentation and/or abuse. Our casual attitudes are being replaced with an informed respect and fear of drug dependence. Most of the population possesses a basic understanding of alcoholism and chemical dependency.

However, the influences of a previous generation are still with us, and it may take another two to three generations to outdistance them. This seems to be a fundamental sociological phenomenon. Once a society realizes a mistake, there is a initial lag in reponse, and then a long struggle to undo the original damage. Recovery from inflation and ensuing recession is a good example of how long the process can take.

Drug abuse has a strong foothold in our society, and preys on those members who are the most vunerable and impressionable. Adolescents are not well defended against the opportunities to try drugs. Unless our culture makes an organized effort to create an immunization process, our children will be exposed to experiences with which they cannot cope.

Chapter 3

Assessing Chemical Dependency

Determining chemical dependency in the adolescent can be a sensitive and difficult task at best, and is usually characterized by ambiguity and inconsistency. As discussed in Chapter One, we know that adolescent behavior can be erratic and unpredictable — even without ingesting chemicals. And so, assessing chemical dependency can become like walking through a maze full of deadends and misleading routes that lead nowhere.

In the recent past, alcohol and drug abuse among adolescents was combined into the broad category of delinquency. It was believed that chemical abuse was just another symptom of delinquent behavior, and treated more as a discipline problem. These behaviors were often considered a manifestation of social outrage, rebellion, a need to become more adult-like, or an expression of inner conflicts (i.e., depression, schizophrenia, etc.). When it came to alcohol and drug addiction, we believed that adolescents were merely experimenters, and could not be addicted. Only adults could become addicted to alcohol and drugs, not anyone under the age of 20. Many have believed that addiction was an age dependent issue/condition, and could develop only after a long period of exposure to a substance. Fortunately, our thinking has begun to change in the last few years.

A widely-used and respected diagnostic instrument is the American Psychiatric Association's Diagnostic and Statistical Manual, Volume III. Although the DSM III now offers more specific criteria regarding substance abuse and its development, it is still quite vague on adolescents. The DSM III indicates that substance abuse may occur in the late teens, but it suggests that it is in the 20's, 30's and 40's that we would expect to see actual dependency problems beginning to surface.

Including the DSM III, there are many other commonly used diagnostic instruments/methods. Many of these instruments rely upon traditional methodologies and criteria which may, or may not, be applicable to the adolescent. The common ones are: *The Essentials of Chemical Dependency* by Robert and Mary McAuliffe (1975), *The Michigan Alcoholism Screening Test,* The National Council on Alcoholism's criteria for the diagnosis of alcoholism, *The Jellineck Curve, The Continuous Data Questionnaire* by Poley, Lea and Vibe (1979), and *The Continuum Model* suggested by Lawson, Ellis and Rivers (1984). Each of these models offer useful and relatively clear criteria for the diagnosis of chemical dependency. Besides the models mentioned here, there are numerous questionnaires, checklists, and other instruments with which individual clinicians and treatment centers are experimenting with as diagnostic tools. There exists a need for a scientific and standardized instrument which can be used with reasonable reliability to diagnose adolescent dependency.

The Chemical Dependency Adolescent Assessment Project (1983) of Minneapolis, Minnesota is currently standardizing the results of a three-year study of assessment methods and criteria. This project will hopefully add considerable information to the understanding of adolescent chemical dependency. Although it is not possible to present any of the Project's findings at this time, some of their preliminary hunches will be incorporated into this chapter.

Adolescent chemical dependency assessment is still a relatively uncharted realm. The practitioner must rely upon a variety of methods and criteria in order to gain an accurate impression. The landmarks are far and few between, and the map only offers a vague sense of direction. This chapter will utilize what is known today, and combine this with wise experience to present a method for the counselor to use. The method is not foolproof, but if followed diligently, should bring the counselor some reasonably reliable conclusions.

The First Step

When the clinician begins to tackle the problem of diagnosing the adolescent, he can stumble on the very first question. Can an adolescent be dependent, "addicted," to a chemical substance? All of us, whether we are parents or not, can feel a strong desire to protect a child from the harsh realities of adult life. Children are pressured to grow up rapidly in our society and we adults may want to slow down the process any way we can. It is disconcerting to see a child having to contend with problems which are generally reserved for "adults only." And so, we may balk at the thought of a 13-year-old being chemically dependent, and search for some other explanation. This caution is wise, because it could be all too easy to swing the other way, and label all unacceptable behavior as chemically dependent. However, the chemical dependency counselor has to sort out the subtle differences between true dependency and other life adjustment problems. It is common for parents and other helping professionals to become distracted by acting-out behaviors, and completely miss the adolescent's drug and alcohol abuse. If the chemical abuse is noted, it is frequently misdiagnosed as experimentation, or a symptom of some other problem of more importance. Naturally, parents and counselors may tend toward avoiding the unpleasant possibility of dependency. Much of our society is still shocked to learn of drug-addicted children. If parents were to recognize that their child was addicted to drugs, it would be devastating to their own self respect, to say nothing of their child's "ruined" future!

The counselor's diagnostic skills must be razor sharp, in order to cut through the real substance of the adolescent's difficulty. With this population, even diagnosing life problems can be difficult and elusive. While surveying a wide cross-section of clinicians, it was found that rather vague diagnostic categories were frequently assigned to adolescents presented for therapy. When no clear cut symptoms are forthcoming, the DSM III category of situational disorder is most often assigned. Situational disorder is defined in the DSM III as:

> This major category is reserved for a more or less transient disorder... that occurs in individuals without any apparent underlying mental disorder and represents an acute reaction to overwhelming environmental stress... If the patient has good adaptive capacity his symptoms usually recede as the stress diminishes. (P. 000)

Adolescents receive the diagnosis of situational disorder at a rate five times more often than do adults (U.S. Department of HEW, 1969). In studying this phenomenon further, we find that situational disorders are not necessarily a common pattern of adolescent disorders, but that the category is more likely overused. As mentioned above, clinicians are reluctant to label a given adolescent behavior as pathological, when there is some doubt that is may be situational in nature. It is generally true that most adolescent difficulties are situational and will be short-lived. But, to assign this diagnosis simply because we are unsure could be life-threatening to the chemically dependent young person. There is a need for a method of accurately identifying adolescent behavior problems, and, more specifically, chemical dependency.

Frequently, the parent of the adolescent will deny that there may be any problem with alcohol and drugs, and will hesitate before bringing the child to see a professional. Clinical experience has shown that once a parent has delivered the teenager for an assessment, it is for a good reason. It is rare that parents jump too quickly to bring in their child (although early intervention is the best measure of prevention). It is most often the case that there is sufficient evidence of a drug problem to warrant an evaluation. When the parents bring in their child, it is only after they have argued at great lengths over their adolescent, and what should be done about his behavior, before seeking help. In families where the parents are chemically dependent, the delay before bringing the child will be even longer. The evaluation is potentially threatening to the parent's use. Long-term denial and avoidance can be an early indication of a general deterioration at home, as is the case in many chemically dependent family systems (Forrest, 1983).

Chemical Dependency: A Definition

Offering a definition of chemical dependency is not as easy as in other disease processes, and this is due, in part, to the heavy influence of socialization. In Lawson (et. al. 1984), chemical dependency is defined as a series of complex interactions between people, their environment and the chemical they choose to use. These "complex interactions" are characterized by a steady deterioration of one's lifestyle and health. Chemical dependency should be viewed as a continuum of progressively dysfunctional states. The type of person, his/her environment, the chemical involved and the pattern of use should all be considered in the diagnosis of the patient.

The National Council on Alcoholism suggests the following major indicators:

1. The presence of physical tolerance or a withdrawal syndrome.

2. Inappropriate continuation of an unhealthy and dangerous pattern of use after the hazard has been identified.

3. The presence of physical disease that is drug related.

4. The person's conviction that he cannot control his use of chemicals.

If any of these factors are present, it can be an indication of dependency. However, none of these indicators may show up in the chemically dependent adolescent. Adolescent chemical dependency often goes undetected in adolescents because they must use chemicals secretly. In most environments, it is unacceptable for young people to use alcohol or drugs openly. And so, it is usually only the adolescent and his peers who have any knowledge of physical tolerance, or the continuation of a dangerous pattern. Peers are generally an unreliable source of information, because they may be poorly informed, or biased in their observations. Determining dependency in the adolescent cannot rely on the identification of a brief list of specific symptoms. Rather, we need to approach this task as a process whereby we collect a wide cross-section of information from several sources.

When defining chemical dependency in relation to adolescents, we must work with broader terms that emphasize behavioral and social characteristics. Robert and Mary McAuliffe offer some helpful descriptions that can be used in assessing the adolescent. The McAuliffes' emphasize that chemical dependency is a "pathological relationship between a person and a mood-altering chemical substance, with the expectation of a rewarding experience (McAuliffe, 1975)." It is the repeating of this rewarding experience, in spite of obvious harmful effects, that distinguishes dependency from abuse. On an occassional basis, an adolescent may ingest drugs and experience harmful effects. Yet, when the young person repeatedly seeks this experience and disregards the negative consequences, dependency probably has occurred. So in a sense, it is not the substance that the adolescent becomes dependent upon, but the rewarding experience itself. This leads to a personal and committed relationship with the drug and a set of symptoms may begin to emerge. Some of the symptoms could be:

1. A psychological dependency, or need.
2. Mental obsession with drugs and their rewards.
3. An emotional compulsion to ingest drugs.
4. Diminished ego strength and apathy for activities which were once important to the individual.
5. Rigid/negative feelings and attitudes.
6. A rigid defense system.
7. Distorted perceptions of self and the environment.
8. Inability to recognize one's condition.

The symptoms listed above are taken from the work of the McAuliffe's. An aspect of the McAuliffes' model which is helpful with adolescents is that they do not require the presence of physical addiction to be dependent. This model focuses upon the user's relationship with the drug and how it affects him. It is the psycho-physical changes in mood, feeling and mind that the person becomes dependent upon. And so, this, in part, explains the adolescent's rejection of the notion that he could be dependent upon a substance. Since they do not typically experience withdrawal, adolescents do not perceive dependency in the traditional, or physical sense. The adolescent believes the psychophysical changes to be positive in nature, as well as reinforcing, and this leads to the continued use.

Some caution should be used when referring to the eight symptoms listed above. Symptoms 4 through 8 can be observed in the non-dependent youth, and their existence alone does not indicate dependency. Adolescents experiencing developmental changes in identity, values and ego can demonstrate any of those symptoms. All adolescents at times will experience apathy. All adolescents will exhibit rigid/negative attitudes. All adolescents at times will be rigidly defensive. A natural condition of adolescence is a distorted and overly self-conscious perception of self and the environment. And finally, all adolescents will at times be unable to recognize changes in their behavior, and that they are being totally unreasonable. It is the first three symptoms and how they superimpose themselves upon the other five, and all other phases of development, that are of concern to the diagnostician.

To summarize, it could be said that a definition of chemical dependency would involve the continued use of a drug, and the experiencing of repeated life problems due to this use. Has the pattern of drug use gained dominance of the young person's life, and is it beyond his/her ability to control? This broad definition gives the counselor a frame of reference within which to work, but is not so confining that it forces a rigid set of criteria.

Initiating the Process

When beginning the assessment process, the counselor must have a clear sense of what elements he is looking for. This requires an ability to know the difference between use, abuse, and dependency. The adolescent could be anywhere along this continuum and move around from time to time. But, it is generally possible to identify certain characteristics in the person's usage that will assign them to one category or another.

An adolescent who uses alcohol and drugs, but is not abusive or dependent, does so in a manner that is purposeful and "appropriate." This immediately raises two questions: What is purposeful use? And, what is appropriate use? An addicted person uses substances purposefully, to become intoxicated and maintain the addiction. But, this is not an appropriate use. Purpose and appropriateness must go hand in hand. Adolescents must know why and how they will use drugs and alcohol prior to the planned use. And, they must reconcile themselves to never abandoning their moral values while under the influence, or never allow use to get beyond their ability to control. For instance: Before going to a party where alcohol will be available, John decides in advance he will only drink one beer to be "sociable" (i.e. to fit in with the group).

This notion of "appropriateness" is a delicate one. There is a very fine line between appropriate use and abuse for the adolescent who chooses to use substances at all. This is because adolescents have no prior experience with alcohol and drug use. They have no frame of reference to rely upon. If you have never been intoxicated before, it is difficult to gauge the relative effect the substance is having upon you. The mature and well disciplined youth may be so purposeful in his use that he never allows himself more than a few sips of beer out of fear of drunkeness. However, most adolescents are more impulsive than this, and will tend not to monitor the effect of their ingestion as closely. This may result in an occasional over-indulgence, followed immediately by guilt and remorse. This would be characterized as an incidence of abuse. Generally speaking, use would be under control and limited by the person's intentions and the situation.

It is not the intention of the author to suggest that adolescents should ever use alcohol or drugs. But, the reader should possess some sense of what is normal use for the drug, alcohol.

Abuse would occur when the drugs are ingested in an inappropriate (irresponsible) manner and result in some harm, or injury to the abuser, or others. This may be accidental, or intentional, such as the boy who intends to get drunk because his girlfriend has dumped him. Harm could be defined by something as simple as a hangover, and/or a mother having to clean up her daughter's vomit in the middle of the night. The child who then confesses to his/her abuse and learns his/her limits from the experience is not likely to become dependent. But, the child who denies any use at all and lies about what happened, may be in the early stages of a budding dependency just waiting to happen. If the parent cooperates in this denial, ignoring their observations (vomit on the bedroom carpet after an evening out), then this may be the beginnings of a "co-dependency."

Chemical use among adolescents cannot be viewed in isolation from other factors. The counselor must collect information about all aspects of the young person's use, health, family, peers, school environment, and heredity. Also, the counselor must be well versed in adolescent development, so as to put into proper context a given set of behaviors and their relationship to other factors in an individual's life. A 12-year-old's experimenting with drugs should be considered as more serious than a 16-year-old who confesses to drinking at a friend's party. Also, children of alcoholic parents who experiment with drugs are the cause for more concern than for children from non-alcoholic homes.

ASSESSMENT IN CONTEXT

Any thorough assessment must reflect the totality of an individual's experience and given situation. Addressing only the chemical use history and current use is particularly irresponsible when evaluating an adolescent. The counselor must ask himself what this given adolescent's use of drugs means in the context of his entire life. Is his use/abuse related to some other situation going on within the family? Is there a history of drug abuse by the parents? Is there a current crisis? The counselor must begin the evaluation assuming he knows nothing about the client's situation, or why the client came for an evaluation. The following is a list of categories to be investigated:

1. Family history: What family factors may put the adolescent at risk for chemical dependency?

2. Social relationships: How have the adolescent's friendships changed, who do they spend time with and what are their social skills?

3. School functioning: How has the young person's performance changed at school, has it deteriorated, are they absent a lot, etc.?

4. Personality changes: Does the individual seem especially moody, lethargic, oppositional, indifferent, secretive, or defensive?

5. Anti-social behavior: Does the adolescent seem to have repeated conflicts with authority figures and the community in general?

6. Personal appearance: How has the adolescent's mode of dress and personal hygiene changed?

7. Availability: Does the adolescent seem distant and frequently absent from home?

8. Sexual activity: When did the adolescent have their first sexual experience and what is their current functioning?

9. Evidence of drug use: Has the youth been caught using drugs, has paraphennalia been found, does he minimize his use, deny his use?

When an adolescent is brought to a counselor for an assessment of a drug problem, it is not (usually) because he is experimenting. It is generally fair to assume that the adolescent has been using drugs, and this behavior has come to the attention of someone. Being able to distinguish the difference between abuse and dependency is critical at this point in the process of evaluation. The case of Ted is a good example.

Ted is a 15-year-old high school sophomore with a drinking problem. The problem is that every time Ted drinks, he does so until he becomes "blind drunk." Ted reports an inability to stop drinking when he starts. Ted does not intend to get drunk, in fact, he always only intends to drink "one or two beers." But every time Ted drinks the same thing happens — he gets drunk. Ted has only consumed alcohol on five occasions! The pattern of drinking looks like alcoholic drinking, yet after only five occasions could we accurately diagnose Ted as alcoholic? Further investigation is indicated. Upon looking deeper, we find a healthy home environment, a good student, an active social life, many other activities which do not involve alcohol, and no evidence of dependency in the family background. There are no other indications of deterioration in Ted's life, as we would expect to find in the dependent person. It would seem that Ted's use of alcohol is abusive, and he is unable to control it. It is obvious that the solution is for Ted to stop consuming alcohol, and not try any other drugs either. If Ted were to continue his use of alcohol, it is very likely that serious consequences would follow.

Ted's problem was caught early, and is an example of an abusive use of alcohol. Ted did not seek to get intoxicated, but quickly found himself unable to control his use of alcohol. Ted and his family could benefit from educational counseling on alcohol and drugs, but more intensive treatment is not indicated. Ted must abstain from alcohol though, it is probably wise to avoid it until he is an adult, and then be very careful if he should decide to try it again.

Assigning the diagnosis of chemical dependency more often than not requires an extensive assessment. This process is further complicated by resistance encountered with the adolescent and sometimes the entire family. The next case example demonstrates a more typical evaluation of a 15-year-old girl.

Case Example: Iron Maiden

Sharon was the antithesis of what one would expect of a "typical" 15-year-old girl from a middle class home. Sharon's constant uniform was a pair of ragged Levi's, a dark t-shirt with the insignia of the Iron Maiden rock group on the front, and an old, faded denim jacket. Sharon's make-up added to her "hard" image, with heavy eye shadow and a pale complexion. Sharon's facial expression seemed blank and distant, with little or no expression of emotion. In every way, Sharon was the Iron Maiden.

Sharon was referred for a chemical dependency evaluation by the juvenile court because she had been picked up as a minor in possession of alcohol. Sharon's family was required to attend the assessment interview, also. Sharon's mother is a woman in her late 30's, well-dressed in a business suit, and seated next to her younger daughter, Kelly. Kelly is 12, and was sort of leaning on Mom, with one leg draped over Mom's lap. Kelly was dressed in neat jeans and a button-down oxford blouse. Sharon's father sat on the other side of the waiting room next to Sharon. Sharon's father is also in his late 30's, and dressed in a dark grey business suit.

During the interview, the parents presented themselves as friendly and articulate. Both parents are professional people who are committed to their careers, and openly admitted that there were occasional conflicts over juggling the two careers and a family. Both children were quiet, looked down at the floor, and responded minimally to the interviewer's questions. The parents volunteered that Kelly was an excellent student and had never caused them any trouble, although they did feel she could be a little more outgoing and sociaable. "Sharon is another story," said the mother as she looked at her eldest daughter.

The father broke in then, "Yes, we have been concerned about Sharon for some time. She seems more sullen and moody all the time, and we are unable to get her to talk to us about anything." Sharon continued to sit silent and stare at the floor. Kelly moved her chair closer to Mom and looked provocatively innocent.

"Sharon seems to want nothing to do with her family. Sometimes I look at her and I don't even know her anymore," the mother shared, with a pained expression on her face.

It appeared to the counselor that Sharon was, in fact, a peripheral member of the family. It also appeared that the umbilical cord between Mother and Kelly had somehow been overlooked and was still attached. As the conversation went on, it seemed that the father was slightly more involved with Sharon, and made more effort to reach out to her.

As the interview progressed, the parents shared that Sharon's school performance had never been outstanding, but there were some courses that did interest her, and in those she would do above average work. However, in the last few months Sharon was not even trying in the courses she liked. Sharon was on the verge of failing every class, and had the maximum amount of allowable absences before she would be suspended. On more than one occasion, Sharon had received detentions at school for smoking cigarettes in the bathroom, arguing with teachers, and going off school grounds without a pass.

When asked what she felt about school, Sharon said, "I hate it, and it's a waste of time. Besides, all the teachers are jerks and don't know anything anyway!" When asked about future plans, Sharon indicated with a shrug that she had none.

According to the parents, Sharon had completely changed her circle of friends and none of the old friends came around the house anymore. As a matter of fact, the parents did not really know who Sharon's friends were. She was vague and secretive about them. Also, Sharon was secretive about what she did and where she went with her friends. When the parents would try tp inquire about Sharon's plans for the evening, they would always end up in a shouting match, and it became easier to just let her go. "Since her arrest, we have decided to crack down, and she can't go out at all now," the mother said with anger in her voice.

Suddenly, Sharon raised up on her chair and exclaimed in a firm voice, "It's none of your business where I go and what I do. I'm almost 16 and can take care of myself. I don't need you to baby me like you do Kelly." A look of utter disgust came over Sharon's face as she looked at her sister seated across from her.

"Well, just a minute, young lady," interjected Dad. "You proved you can't be trusted, and it is our responsibility to know your whereabouts at all times, particularly now that you are on probation. If we don't keep track of you, we will be in trouble with the court too."

At this point, the interviewer interrupted the interchange to return to the task of collecting information. It was apparent that Sharon had a considerable amount of power in the family, and now was not the time to get into this issue, or the interview would just deteriorate.

The counselor then learned that Sharon was generally distant and avoided interacting with the rest of the family at home. Sharon was short-tempered and intolerant of Kelly, and frequently accused the parents of favoring her. Kelly was, in fact, more popular with her parents, and caused them few, if any problems. Sharon would fly into a rage if anyone, but especially Kelly, ever came into her room uninvited, or disturbed any of her possessions. To some extent, the parents believed this was normal sibling rivalry and tried their best to mediate the conflicts. However, Sharon always felt she was being "ganged up on" and was not treated fairly. At this point, Sharon would usually storm out of the house and not come back for hours, and on a few occasions would stay away overnight.

Another way Sharon would not participate at home was when she would come home and go straight to bed. Sharon seemed exhausted much of the time, and would sleep an inordinate amount, at all times of the day. She rarely ate meals with the family, and when she did it was usually unpleasant for everyone. To her parents, Sharon seemed self-centered, demanding, aloof, impulsive, secretive, restless, depressed, disorganized and sloppy. Sharon also seemed pre-occupied with sex, drugs and rock'n'roll, or at least the posters on her bedroom wall indicated that. Sharon constantly listened to music that promoted rebellion, violence and a general anti-social attitude. The parents struggled with whether all the characteristics were a normal stage of adolescent rebellion, or indications of a more serious problem. On one occasion, Sharon's mother did ask her if she had ever used drugs. "She told me she tried pot once and had drank a can of beer once at a party, but that was all," said the mother. "I believed her then, but now I'm not sure."

During the assessment interview, the mother admitted to having an alcoholic father and a very unpleasant childhood. She avoided alcohol herself for that very reason. The father denied any alcohol problem, but when his wife was interviewed alone she disclosed that she was concerned about his drinking. "He never gets really drunk, it just seems that he has 4 to 6 drinks almost every evening, and then goes to bed. He doesn't drink like my dad did," the wife pointed out.

Both parents emphasized that they did not believe Sharon was chemically dependent, but that she had probably been influenced by some of her friends. "Sharon just isn't the type of child to get involved with drugs on her own."

Looking at this family from the outside, there are numerous problems that can be identified. Clearly, Sharon is exhibiting the most disturbed behavior within the family. Some clinicians might believe that Sharon's behavior is typical of an adolescent adjustment problem. It is not uncommon for adolescents to appear self-centered, demanding, etc. Sharon could even be diagnosed as experiencing a "situational disorder" and will probably grow out of it. The therapist who is untrained in chemical dependency might conclude the assessment at this point and begin therapy with the family. However, if the counselor were to continue to pursue the alcohol and drug issue, she might uncover additional information.

After excusing the rest of the family from the room, the counselor interviewed Sharon alone. At first the conversation focused upon general and non-threatening topics, such as school and parents. Then in a matter of fact way the counselor said, "I need to ask you some questions about your drug use history." At this juncture the counselor must ask direct and open-ended questions, eliminating the possibility of only yes-no answers. Some sample questions might be:

— *Tell me about when you first tried drugs.*

— *What was it like when you first got high?*

— *How did you keep your parents from knowing when you were high?*

Generally, an adolescent will give helpful answers to these questions. The questions assume drug use, and do not put the child in a position of having to deny, or defend his/her use. Later in this chapter, a more complete list of questions will be presented.

While interviewing Sharon privately, she revealed that she had first used marijuana when she was 12. Sharon believed this was not harmful to her, and that all of her friends were trying it too. When asked if all of her friends had continued to use marijuana, Sharon said, "No, just one friend and I kept on using. The others chickened out." After a lengthy interview about her drug use history, Sharon revealed that she had: used drugs in solitude; concealed her drug use; felt anxious when she ran out of drugs; experimented with a variety of drugs; made social plans according to the availability of drugs; felt better about herself when she was high; increased her tolerance for alcohol; tried to quit using a couple of times; had taken extra drugs along to a party just in case; lied about her hangovers; and, basically did not like herself.

This information, and that provided by Sharon's parents, seems to indicate that her deterioration and drug abuse were probably related. In this case there seems to be sufficient information to warrant the diagnosis of chemical dependency for Sharon. All of the data considered collectively paints a rather classic picture to the trained eye. It would be expected for any adolescent to exhibit some of the problems seen in Sharon, but not all of them. There seems to be some underlying pathology, because too many things were going wrong in Sharon's life. Even though there may have been other family problems, including marital ones, Sharon was in need of the immediate attention. A swift and direct intervention upon Sharon's pattern of drug use was necessary.

Sharon's dependency had reached a point where she was using drugs to feel normal. Her outward behavior was beginning to resemble anything but normal, yet Sharon's parents were reluctant to investigate. The situation was declining rapidly, and no one knew what to do about it. The parents questioned their own judgment, and Sharon's thinking was becoming progressively less reliable and more delusional. Continued chemical dependency treatment was essential.

Once a thorough assessment had been conducted upon Sharon, the diagnosis of chemical dependency became clear. Yet, in many cases it becomes more difficult for the evaluator to reach as clear a conclusion. The following case is an example of just such a problem:

Example 2: Short in Stature

Billy was short and hated it. At 16 he was still only 5'3", and there were no signs he would get any taller. Both of Billy's parents were short too, and this was not very encouraging for him either. His father was a successful architect who traveled to construction sites all over the world. Billy's mother was a housewife, and stayed home to take care of him and his younger sister and brother. Billy had one older brother who was living on his own after dropping out of high school in the 10th grade. Billy's parents were married later in life, and so he found himself with a 60-year-old father who was looking forward to retirement and his easychair. Billy's primary interaction with Dad was to ask for the car keys or money. Billy and his mother interacted often, and at a decibel level which could be heard by most of the neighbors. Neither of Billy's parents had any history of alcoholism in their individual, or family backgrounds.

Billy was not a dishonest kid, he just manipulated the truth. This means that he would tell the truth if asked the right question in the right way. Billy had aspirations of becoming a lawyer, and seemed to possess some of the necessary prerequisites. Unfortunately, Billy's grades in school were terrible. He was always on the brink of passing or failing most every class. Usually, he would pass and be advanced to the next grade level, but by the skin of his teeth. Billy's charming personality at school would generally get him through difficulties.

Billy was referred by the school counselor for a chemical dependency evaluation because he was caught coming on campus intoxicated. It was the school's policy to temporarily suspend students for this offense until they could prove they had sought professional help. Once Billy and his parents had completed the evaluation, then he could return to school.

During the assessment interview, Billy sat casually, dressed in his "preppy" outfit, with a blank look on his face. The mother was polite, talkative and lead the preliminary conversations. The father looked tired, but impeccably dressed, and offered nothing unless asked. The mother was clearly the social agent for the family.

Billy's 13-year-old sister and 8-year-old brother were also present. The younger brother, Matt, sat next to his mother and periodically would kick at Billy's feet. Billy would give him such a glare of hate that one would think Matt could have fried on the spot. The 13-year-old, Trisha, sat very properly and quietly, but would return glances to Billy identical to those he had directed at Matt. Throughout all of this non-verbal barrage, mother continued to talk nonstop about her family as if at a bridge party.

"Billy has always been popular at school," volunteered the mother. "But at home his attitude is distinctly sour and oppositional. Billy and Trisha seem to hate each other, and he tolerates Matt."

When the father was asked for his opinion about Billy, he said, "We do not expect excellent grades from Billy, just average, but he can't seem to do even that." With some coaxing, the father went on to share about how Billy hated school, and how he could never make it in the real world with that attitude.

At this point, Billy interrupted to say, "I will do better in school if you and Mom will buy me a new sports car." Billy was always the negotiator and would bargain over almost everything.

As the interview continued, it was learned that Billy was an accomplished manipulator of his parents, and could easily divide them. The parents were rarely in agreement anyway, and so this was an open invitation for Billy to get what he wanted.

Both parents reported being weary of parenting and, as a result, would sometimes avoid decision-making. "We know this is wrong, but sometimes it just seems futile and endless to argue over everything," sighed the mother. As a result of the inconsistent discipline, Billy was frequently able to avoid telling the whole truth. If he just argued long enough about trivial details, he could get most of what he wanted — details such as, "I did too call you at midnight last Tuesday, you just thought it was 1:30."

In this case, as in the previous one, the use of alcohol was the reason for the referral. The mother and father were aware of Billy's drinking, and had seen him come home drunk on more than one occasion. Billy's mother would lecture him about drinking, this would escalate into a shouting match, and the father would finally intervene and tell them both "shut-up." Billy would then go to his room and his parents would argue for another hour or two. Billy would usually escape any consequences this way.

While interviewing Billy alone, he admitted to drinking too much once in a while. "But I don't have a drinking problem. It's my parents who have the problem, not me!" Every time a question was directed to him about his behavior, Billy would attempt to divert it to a discussion about his parents, and how it was all their fault.

After further questioning, Billy did begin to share more about his drinking history. He admitted that he did not like alcohol at first, and it took him a while to acquire a taste for it. "Now I can drink a whole six-pack and still feel pretty good," Billy pronounced with a proud smile. "I feel more relaxed and confident after I have had a few beers, and my friends think I'm funnier too."

To Billy, being accepted by his friends was of the utmost importance. The values of his parents were of no concern to him, or so he reported. It was the stories Billy's friends would tell about him after a drinking episode that caused him to be well known at school. Billy took great pride in being known as "crazy" by the kids at school. It would appear that Billy was stuck in an earlier stage of development. Billy was maturing slowly, and his reputation reinforced him to avoid growing up.

Although Billy admitted to abusing alcohol, he was careful to add that he was not as bad as some of his friends. "I'm no burn-out. At least I know when to quit, and I don't use any other drugs." It appeared that Billy's use of alcohol was utilitarian in nature, that he drank with a purpose in mind. It was not uncommon for Billy's abuse of alcohol to lead to harmful results, but this was his intention, as a way to draw attention to himself.

At the outset, this case might seem suspicious to a chemical dependency counselor. Billy appears to be demonstrating some of the symptoms of dependency. Billy would avoid his parents and siblings at home. His school functioning was poor, but it had always been below average. On the other hand, Billy was popular with his friends and this group had remained fairly stable since elementary school. Also, Billy's personality had always been split, pleasant outside of the home and irritable when at home. Billy was always meticulous about his appearance and tried whatever he could to make himself look taller. There was no evidence of alcoholism on either side of the family. There does not seem to be any general deterioration of Billy's life, but some specific dysfunction related to his alcohol use, combined with ineffectual parenting.

It would appear that Billy is abusing alcohol, but not necessarily dependent on it. As the McAuliffe's suggest, the dependent person has an unhealthy committed relationship with drugs which is compulsive in nature. Billy's use of alcohol seems to be utilitarian. In combination with Billy's slow maturation, the alcohol provides him with a fortified sense of self esteem. Billy did not drink alone, hide alcohol, drink to feel normal, or suffer any significant changes in personality. Billy planned his use, and always with the same purpose in mind — to add to his stature. Billy's abuse of alcohol seems to be related to his inability to adjust to problems in his development, and his parents were unable to help him due to their own problems.

Billy and his parents were clearly in need of therapy, but specific chemical dependency treatment was not indicated. Billy was experiencing trouble dealing with his physical limitations, and was compensating in a potentially dangerous way. Clearly, Billy needed to stop drinking, but his need to compensate for a perceived inadequacy was not abnormal. As described in Chapter One, each adolescent must struggle to develop his own positive self identity. Yet, they are not always well-equipped to be who they feel they should be. Billy was getting positive attention for his "crazy" behavior, and was willing to settle for this. Billy needed his parents and others to help him to discover other positive characteristics within himself.

Again, it is essential to consider the context of the adolescent's situation. What is going on in the rest of his life, why is he using drugs now, and what function do drugs serve in his life? We most likely will never find any "positive" function for the illegal use of drugs for adolescents. The point to understand is the inter-relationship between drugs and other aspects of the young person's life. For some adolescents, drugs become the central focus of their lives and organize all of their behavior. The next case example will describe such an individual.

Case Example 3: The Stunt Man

Richard lived in a world of fantasy, and if the real world had not discovered him, he might still be trapped there. When Richard was born, his mother had just remarried, although not to Richard's father. Richard's new stepfather quickly adopted Richard, and he never knew his real father. Richard's mother had an older son and daughter. Her new husband had several older sons. Richard, his mother and father were the only ones left living at home. Richard was 15 in years, but, in reality, he was far behind his peers in maturity. Richard's father was a respected businessman in the community and spent very little time at home. Richard's mother did her best to care for Richard, but she, too, was distracted by other activities and pursuing her career. For most of his life, Richard was free to come and go as he pleased. Since he never got into any serious trouble, no one thought too much about Richard's whereabouts.

Richard's older sister was chemically dependent, but this was minimized and overlooked by the rest of the family. Richard would spend countless hours at his sister's house. Richard's mother assumed his sister was supervising him, but most of the time she was gone and would leave him in charge of her two small children. This was fertile ground for the development of the problems that were to follow.

Richard spent a great deal of time watching television, reading *Conan the Barbarian*-type books and drawing violent, grotesque pictures. At the age of nine, Richard discovered alcohol, and quickly developed a dependency upon it. The alcohol was easy to obtain at his sister's house, and so it was always available to him. It was not unusual for his sister to come home and find Richard watching television and drinking her beer. Richard's sister thought it was "cute" to see her little brother drunk, but when he started to deplete her supply of beer she put a stop to it. Richard's parents were completely unaware of what was going on.

After Richard's sister discovered he was drinking up all her beer, she decided to introduce him to marijuana. She thought it would be easier to regulate his use of marijuana, because it was easier to hide. Richard immediately discovered a new way to dramatically enhance his fantasy world from the first time he smoked marijuana. And so, for a while, Richard lost interest in beer. Richard's sister was relieved, since marijuana was not harmful like alcohol.

Although his sister thought she was controlling Richard's use of marijuana, he did not take long to discover how to procure it himself. All he had to do was go down to the playground and flash his generous allowance, and in no time he could score some dope. Also Richard discovered a whole new group of friends who also liked to indulge in fantasy. Richard's goal in life was to become a stuntman so he could act out all those fantasies. Marijuana seemed to help all those fantasies seem more real.

As years went by, Richard became completely lost in this world of fantasy and drugs, and no one in his family knew. Progressively, Richard became less discriminating about which drugs he would use. If marijuana was not available, then he would drink alcohol. If alcohol was not available then he would consume whatever he could get his hands on. Being high was a constant state for Richard by the time he was 12. There were many close calls where he could have been detected by adults, but Richard was generally careful about covering his use. Also there was his sister. She could always be counted on to cover for him.

As Richard got older, his tolerance for drugs and alcohol increased, and so did his need for the money to support his dependency. So stealing became the easiest way to acquire the money Richard needed. At first, Richard would steal out of his mother's purse, but that was risky and occasionally he would get caught. Then Richard began stealing stereos out of cars and exchanging them for drugs with his dealer. Sometimes he would sell the stolen property to friends, because the rate of exchange was better that way. Richard was never without money, and at times his parents were suspicious of this, but they would always accept his explanations of how he got it.

Like drugs and fantasy, sex became an early preoccupation for Richard. Sometimes Richard would have sex with girls in exchange for drugs, and other times just for the fun of it. Richard's moral values were dangerously distorted, and he was progressively becoming more controlled by his desire for pleasure. It had become normal for Richard to act out his fantasies and fulfill his desires without any consideration for the consequences. And so, when he began feeling sexual desires for his three-year-old niece, there was little standing between the thought and the act. Richard struggled with the thought for a while, but he was too vulnerable to his own desires, and was unable to resist. Once Richard followed through and forced his niece to have sex with him, it became easier to do it again. He felt compelled to do it again. At this point, Richard began to feel a deep sense of guilt, unlike any he had ever felt before. Richard knew only one way to deal with troublesome feelings, and that was to get high.

Richard was hooked in two ways: He could not resist having sex with his niece, and he was dependent upon drugs to maintain his sense of "reality." Things began to spiral out of control quickly at this point. The more Richard gave in to his incestual desires, the more he had to use drugs to mask the guilt and pain. Richard knew he needed help, but was terrified of what would happen if he confessed what he had done. There seemed no escape from this horrible dilema.

As Richard increased his consumption of drugs, he became careless in his behavior. Usually a carefree and mellow youngster, Richard had now become angry, sullen and occasionally violent. Richard's mood at home became volatile, and he would fly into a rage at the least provocation. His parents were dumbfounded. Richard had never before caused any problem. Granted he was a poor student, but that was excused by what was diagnosed in the first grade as a learning disability. Richard was crying out for help, but his parents were unable to interpret it as such. Unfortunately, Richard's parents had other problems which took up most of their attention. Richard's farter was diagnosed as having heart disease, and was in and out of the hospital. Richard's timing was terrible. The family was simply unable to respond to his need for attention.

It was Richard's carelessness which finally lead to his receiving help. While breaking into a car, he was caught by the police and arrested. He was placed in the juvenile detention center and his mother was notified of the arrest. Then both Richard and his mother were interviewed by the juvenile probation authorities, and he was placed on probation. Richard's father was too ill to come to the interview. Richard was then referred to a counselor for a chemical dependency evaluation.

The evaluator uncovered the story of Richard's drug use history, but not the incest. Richard was transferred to an adolescent treatment center, and there in group therapy he confessed the incest. Although Richard's story may seem extreme, it is not atypical of many stories told in treatment centers. These adolescents' lives have deteriorated so severely, they can no longer function normally in society. Furthermore, their families are unable to cope with the problems, and frequently are completely unaware. The family system is unable to mobilize the necessary resources to effectively intervene upon the member's illness.

The case examples above are representative of a wide cross-section of youth one might expect to see in counseling. To truly determine if the adolescent is chemically dependent or abusing drugs, a thorough case history is necessary. The interviewer must have a clear sense of how to proceed with the assessment. The next section will outline a recommended procedure to follow when conducting an assessment.

Conducting the Assessment

When conducting an assessment interview with an adolescent and his family, it is essential to keep it on a friendly level, as if you were a visitor in their home. The assessment is a very personal intrusion into the life of the family. Most families are quite apprehensive about a "chemical dependency assessment." The attitude and demeanor of the interviewer can have a tremendous impact upon their level of comfort. Before asking the key questions about drug use, the interviewer should ask less threatening questions first, such as: Do both parents work, how long have they been married, how would they assess their situation in life (i.e., income, housing, health, etc.), and how do they feel about coming in for this interview? The interviewer must walk a fine line between appearing as a friendly neighbor and a sensitive clinician. To gain the information needed, the interviewer will have to delve into the soul of the family and each of its members. A blunt and direct approach can prove to be unproductive and put unnecessary distance between the interviewer and the family.

The first collection of information occurs when the mother calls to make the appointment. It is always the mother. An interesting procedure for gaining information at this point is to request that the mother either call the adolescent to the phone, or have him call back to arrange the first appointment. This may appeal to the adolescent's interest in autonomy and self direction. Also, this allows the counselor to find out how the family responds to this assignment. Do they cooperate, does the mother make the appointment anyway, and is the adolescent successful in getting the rest of the family to come to the interview? It is always interesting to see how the adolescent and his family respond to this invitation to maturity.

Obviously, not all adolescents will respond to this call to maturity, and will refuse to have anything to do with an evaluation. But, more frequently, someone else in the family will sabotage the first interview, and generally it is the parents who do so.

To avoid this, the counselor must be explicit in his instructions about who must attend the first session. Experience has shown that if the father is not specifically requested at the first interview, nine times out of ten, he will not show up. Furthermore, the chemically dependent child is usually a powerful member of the family, and parents may have a struggle in getting him/her to come to the interview. They may need some assistance in getting the child to come in.

It is never recommended that parents lie to their child about the nature of the interview. The parents should be honest about why they want to see a counselor. However, the fragile ego of the adolescent may be unable to handle the implication that he/she is the "problem." They may already believe they are the "problem," but will resent having their nose rubbed in it. It is usually helpful for the parents to say, "This family is having problems and your mother and I have decided that we are going to get help."

When the family arrives, it is important for the interviewer to support the parents as the experts on their family. The parents may not feel as if they are in charge, but the interviewer must treat them as if they are. This is one of the first therapeutic interventions, and one which is appropriate during the assessment phase. The parents must regain control of their adolescent, and they need to hear that message from the beginning. This message will be elaborated upon in the treatment chapter.

When conducting an assessment interview, it is advisable to split family members apart from each other and talk with each individually. Information gained through interviewing the family together is important, but there is much to be learned by visiting with each member alone. The influence of the family can be hypnotic to the individual, and he/she may respond differently when alone (Ritterman, 1983). It is usually easier to form a relationship with parents who are more likely to cooperate in giving information about the family and their adolescent. There can be a number of obstacles to overcome in forming a relationship with the drug-using adolescent. The next section will focus on the interviewer-adolescent relationship.

The Adolescent Interview

One of the first tasks to accomplish when assessing the adolecent for chemical dependency is to establish a climate of cooperation. The interviewer may not be able to gain total cooperation initially, but it is essential to strive towards some kind of basic agreement. This initial agreement should be about some issue which is not threatening to the adolescent's defense system. The most fundamental aggreement may be gained by acknowledging that the young person resents being in the interviewer's office. They may feel that they do not have a problem and it is "stupid" to be talking to a counselor. Joining the adolescent on this issue is recommended, rather than challenging him. If one agrees with the adolescent on this issue, then the adolescent will feel more secure in his ability to defend himself. As mentioned in Chapter One, the early adolescent will deny any problems, and will feel intensely threatened by the assessment situation. The middle adolescent is likely to admit problems, but will minimize them and want to avoid further discussion. The individual in late adolescence may admit his contribution to family problems, but will point out that he is an adult and his life is his business.

Establishing this initial agreement is critical in gaining useful information later. Avoiding a battle over control is essential. The evaluator wants information from the adolescent. Therapy comes later, and issues of control can be discussed then, in the presence of the parents.

This beginning process also helps the evaluator in assessing how "in touch" the adolescent is with his feelings. If he rigidly denies feelings of resentment, anger, hostility, and apprehension, even when they are apparent, then this is significant information. The evaluator must check this information against the given age of the adolescent, too. It would be expected that a 13-year-old might deny everything, but not so with the 17-year-old. If the young person is unable, or unwilling, to discuss even the most obvious feelings, this may indicate he is excessively defended against any potential intrusion. The evaluator must respect this barrier, but not give up on trying other less threatening methods of penetrating it. This is where the less experienced interviewer might give up.

Adolescents can be quite effective at defending themselves through silence. When working with this age group, it is not recommended to allow them to remain in silence too long. If they will not talk, then the counselor needs to keep the conversation going, even talking for the adolescent if necessary. Again, the purpose of the interview is to get information. Waiting for the adolescent to speak is a waste of time. The younger adolescent can become confused by silences and misunderstand their meaning.

The 13-year-old may not realize that silence means the counselor is waiting for him to respond. They may begin to fantasize about the counselor's intentions, and become even more withdrawn, particularly if this is their primary defense mechanism. As long as the counselor carries the conversation and acts friendly, there is a good chance the client will eventually relax.

Once an agreement and some minimal comfort are established, then it is time to begin assessing the adolescent's history of drug use. The first obstacle to overcome here is confidentiality. The adolescent has no reason to believe the counselor can be trusted with incriminating information. Even so, the counselor must assert his intention to keep what the adolescent tells him to himself. Again, this is an assessment, and the rules that apply here may not apply later in therapy. It usually helps to add that the counselor does not expect the adolescent to trust him, but that this trust must be earned. This seems to appeal to the adolescent's need to be treated as an adult. Generally, the adolescent is in a position of having to prove he is trustworthy. When the burden of proof is shifted to the counselor, then the adolescent can relax some.

Drug History

It is best to introduce this subject in a matter of fact way, such as, "I want to ask you a few questions about your use of drugs." The evaluator does not want to come across as judgmental, but curious. The evaluator wants to "understand" the adolescent's experience with drugs. Assume the adolescent uses drugs. This way that initial awkward question can be avoided, "Have you ever used any drugs?" Of course they have, or they would not be there for an evaluation!

The questions which follow do not need to be asked in any particular order. Also, it is best to intermix the questions into the conversation, rather than resembling a final exam which will be computer scored. Avoid the Jack Webb style, "Just the facts, please." The questions are as follows:

1. Do you ever seem sensitive, gloomy, depressed, pessmistic, or hypercritical?
2. Do you place value on getting high?
3. Do you use drugs to achieve a rewarding experience?
4. Do you make special efforts to arrange opportunities to get high?
5. Do you make plans based upon the availability of drugs?
6. When-where did you first get high? Who were you with, and what drug(s) did you use?
7. Do you ever use drugs when alone?
8. Do you ever feel that drugs change your personality, and if so, how?
9. Do you manipulate your personal life to accommodate your relationship with drugs?
10. Do you find yourself looking foward to your next opportunity to get high?
11. Do you ever feel anxious when your drug supply is low or depleted?
12. Do you ever store up, or hide drugs?
13. Do you ever find yourself bragging to others about what drugs do for you?
14. What kind of music do you like to listen to, and why?
15. Have you ever concealed your drug use?
16. Do you ever sneak drugs, take extra "hits" on the side where others won't see you?
17. Do you find yourself avoiding painful subjects at home, or with friends?
18. Have you lost interest in activities which were once important to you?
19. Do you find your effectiveness to be diminished at school, in sports, etc.?
20. Do you seem to have trouble remembering things?
21. Do you ever find yourself ingesting drugs in a rapid manner?
22. Do you ever take fortified doses?
23. Do you use drugs impulsively, with no prior intention to get high?
24. Do you ever make abrupt changes in plans in order to use drugs?

25. Would you attend a party where you knew there would be no drugs?
26. Do you ever continue to use drugs even though you feel bad about it?
27. Have you ever attempted to stop using drugs?
28. Have you ever attempted to cut down your use and been unsuccessful?
29. Have you ever expressed sorrow, shame, or apologized for drug-related behavior?
30. Do you often feel depressed?
31. Do you ever feel suicidal?
32. Are you suspicious and intolerant of others?
33. Do you ever feel like you are going crazy?
34. Has your tolerance for drugs increased, or decreased?
35. Have any of your friends ever told you they felt you got high too much?
36. Is your drug use the same, more, or less than your friends?
37. Have you ever stolen money or other things in order to buy drugs?
38. Have you ever been violent towards anyone in your family?
39. Do you find that you frequently contradict yourself?
40. Do you feel that your parents demand too much from you?
41. Have you ever had one of your parents call your school when you were too hungover to go?
42. Have others accused you of being self-centered and grandiose?
43. Do you have trouble trusting members of your family?
44. Do you have hostile feelings for the authority figures in your life?
45. Do you feel more in control when you are high?

Many of the questions listed above have been adapted from the work of Robert and Mary McAuliffe (1975), as well as Gary Forrest (1983).

It is common, and frequently necessary, when interviewing adolescents, to define terms as clearly as possible. The adolescent must understand what is being asked of him and elaboration is often necessary. The questions should become catalysts to further information, and so the manner in which the questions are asked is critical. A friendly and informal approach seems to work best.

When reviewing the adolescent's and the family's responses, the evaluator will be looking for patterns. Is there a consistent pattern of response to the adolescent's acting out and drug abuse? Does the family ignore the problem, deny it, escalate, or contribute to it? Finally, does the family seem to be dependent upon this pattern and unable to give it up (e.g. is the family dependent upon the adolescent's drug abuse?).

Outpatient vs Inpatient Treatment

When weighing out all the information the evaluator must then determine which treatment environment is most appropriate. Having some clear criteria for making this decision is helpful. The questions listed below can help the couselor decide how best to treat the individual and his family, once the evaluation is completed.

1. What is the best level of psychological development achieved by the adolescent? If the adolescent seems to be severely behind in his development, then inpatient may be contraindicated. The profoundly immature adolescent will not do well in a typical inpatient treatment center, because the intensity will be more than he can cope with. Ego strength is a significant factor to consider.

2. What kind of object relationship has the adolescent established, especially with his parents? As mentioned before, the counselor should expect a fair amount of alienation from the parents, and a strong pull towards the peer group. However, the chemically dependent adolescent is frequently characterized by grossly unrealistic perceptions and expectations of peers and parents.

3. Why is the adolescent showing up for counseling now? Has the adolescent always shown maladaptive behavior, or is this a recent development? Does the disturbance seem to be a reaction to a recent situation, or event? Is the adolescent victimized by specific developmental stresses? The disturbance may be due to the onset of new tasks, specific to a stage of development.

4. Does the adolescent admit to a conflict? If the adolescent does not acknowledge a problem, and consistently denies any drug abuse, then this can become a barrier to outpatient counseling. Does the adolescent truly see no problem, is he too deluded to acknowledge a disturbance, or is he trying to bluff his way out of trouble?

5. Does the adolescent have the capacity to view himself with reasonable objectivity? Some defensiveness and distortions are to be expected, as well as self-protective maneuvers. Some adolescents are simply too well guarded against intrusion by an adult, and need the pressure of the peer group to gain some objectivity. This, generally, can only be found in a residential program with peer therapy groups.

6. Will the adolescent's family permit him to change? The adolescent who previously had functioned at age-appropriate levels, and has achieved fairly gratifying object relationships probably has the capacity, if given proper assistance, and if his family can allow it, to utilize outpatient counseling productively. If the family itself is severely dysfunctional, and needs the adolescent to remain in his "sick" role, then inpatient treatment may be required.

Utilizing the process comfortably will take some practice. There are no crisp, clear answers when assessing for chemical dependency in the adolescent. Also, this process cannot be completed in a one-hour session. Two or three sessions are recommended to get a complete picture.

Once the assessment is complete, the counselor must then share with the family his impressions and recommendations. It is important to be specific at this time. The counselor does not want to appear vague or unsure. If the adolescent has an unhealthy and committed relationship with drugs, then the counselor must tell this to the parents, and what it means. If the adolescent is abusing drugs and at-risk for further problems, then the counselor must elaborate on what this implies. It is never recommended to suggest that an adolescent's drug use is of no concern and can be overlooked. At no time should a counselor support teenage drug use.

The parents and the adolescent must be appraised of the differences between use, abuse and dependency. Treatment recommendations will be determined according to the youngster's level of abuse/dependency. Ted and his family would most likely benefit from an educational type of approach. Sharon and her family would benefit from intensive outpatient counseling. But, if Sharon did not improve, then inpatient treatment should be considered. Sharon's family seems to be relatively intact and functional, and possesses the resources to help her. In the case of Billy, he and his parents needed outpatient family counseling and would also benefit from some alcohol education. Richard was in need of immediate inpatient treatment, because his personal life had deteriorated too far, and the family was unable to mobilize the necessary resources to help him.

Contributing Factors

When an adolescent presents himself for assessment of drug abuse problems, it is entirely possible there are other significant problems waiting in the wings. The drug abuse may be only the tip of the iceberg, and further investigation may reveal deeper more serious problems. On the other hand, the assessment may reveal nothing but and overindulgent youngster and protective parents. It is suggested that clinicians should be as prepared to diagnose no problem as much as they would actual disturbed behavior (Steinberg, 1983). Disturbed behaviors are often sustained by the adolescent's situation, and this should make one circumspect in diagnosing individual disorders.

The child's drug abuse may be a symptom of other familial dysfunctions, or it may mean very little in the context of his situation. It is important to consider that families influence normal behavior, problematic feelings, and psychotic disorders almost in equal proportions. Whatever the adolescent's situation, it is safe to assume the family has had some kind of influence upon it. Others, such as clergy, teachers and juvenile court officers can add helpful information to the diagnosis.

Many times a family that has been referred for an evaluation due to their member's drug use may perceive no problem. However, referral for treatment or evaluation becomes, in itself, a problem for the family. This outside threat may organize a family response that may appear to be defensive and in denial of "the problem." "The problem" is relative to one's point of view. The counselor may see the adolescent's drug use as the problem, and the family may see the counselor as its only problem.

The first chapter emphasizes how the counselor must pay attention to the difference between a developmental disorder and a disease process (dependency). A disorder is, in part, determined by an individual's abnormal functioning. A disease is some psychological, or psychophysical process of disorganization which has become superimposed upon development (Steinberg, 1983). This distinction between disease process and disorder is not always clear. We all, at some time, experience a developmental disorder. This is when our experience and abilities lag behind the immediate demands of a new developmental task. Learning to drive can be a frustrating experience, and we may become depressed over our poor performance. But, after repeated practice, we finally master the new skill. A disease process would impair our ability to approach the new task, and result in an all-encompassing response, such as getting intoxicated because we did not believe we could learn to drive.

Family conflict can certainly influence normal adolescent development, and lead to behavior disorders. Drug abuse may be a manifestation of the famliy conflict, yet the conflict may not be isolated to just this one area. The drug abuse problem may be the only one the family is willing to present. It is then the clinicians job to look at this symptom in its relationship to other family dynamics. Is the drug abuse related to other issues, or is it, in fact, a degenerative process superimposed over normal development?

Steinberg (1983) questions the practice of identifying the adolescent as "patient," when many family therapists repeatedly refer to the family system as the patient. Should there not be some consistency here, such as admitting the entire family as the patient for treatment? The traditional medical model leans toward the individual as the patient, and focuses upon treating his/her symptoms. The counselor assessing the adolescent for chemical dependency can be lured into this same trap. Family therapist Michele Ritterman (1983) refers to the family as offering up the patient as a "gift" to the therapist. The therapist is obliged to accept the gift, but invites the rest of the family to enter into therapy too.

When constructing a diagnostic structure, we need to start with the internal forms and work outward from there. Eventually we come up with a constellation of factors which allows us to see how the entire system is built. When assessing adolescent disorders/diseases, we must first identify the internal structures and then move outward, as follows:

1. Temperamental characteristics; abnormalities underlying psychotic illness; neurological disorders, minor and major disorders of physical health and ability.
2. Intellectual level and specific disabilities and developmental problems.
3. Hypotheses about unconscious conflicts and their effects upon conscious thoughts, feelings and behaviors.
4. Personal beliefs, hopes, fears, ambitions and attitudes.
5. Self-presentations and social skills, obsessive-compulsive behavior, mannerisms and stereotypes.
6. Patterns of feeling and communication within the family.
7. Influences of local peer groups and schools, availability of jobs and recreational facilities.
8. Local laws, rules, customs and practices.

Consider how these factors might impact upon the family in the following case example.

Case Example 4:

A woman with painful and disruptive experiences in her earlier family life marries an unstable, immature man who manages to impress her in defiance of her parent's wishes. Bad feeling surrounds the marriage, and it is assumed by the mother and father that any children, as well as the marriage, will be difficult: hence, a preconceived notion of how things will be. A son is born into this environment where turmoil is already a way of life. The mother smokes heavily and the father drinks heavily, and the advice of the prenatal clinic is ignored. Already, before birth, there are factors operating against the welfare of the child's development. When he starts school, he is the one with poor organizational skills, lives in a low-income neighborhood with other low academic achievement children, and little discipline. Like his father, he is not very bright, but in addition, has a particular difficulty in reading. These were largely inherited vulnerabilities, which could be overcome by skilled teachers, particularly if the parents were members of the articulate and informed middle class. But, neither the parents nor the teachers are concerned about the boy's difficulties, especially his behavior pattern of withdrawal, misery and apathy.

In adolescence, he begins to develop physically and sexually somewhat belately, and his poor social skills and inept role models results in inappropriate handling of aggressive and sexual feelings. This leads him to delinquent behavior, and eventual arrest by the police. His father, who has managed to avoid arrest for years, is angry at the boy's behavior and is drawn into fights with him, particularly when they are both drunk. This eventually leads to a referral for psychiatric treatment for the boy.

Is drug abuse the primary problem of the boy described above? It is apparent that he is experiencing a myriad of troubles, only one of which is drug abuse. This is an example of a systemic disorder where the drug abuse could be a reasonable response to the present situation. Placing the boy in a treatment center for one of his problems may be indicated, but if that were all that was done, he would be guaranteed to fail. A cooperative effort between the parents, the teacher, caseworkers, probation officer and judges would be essential if the child is to succeed. It may not be appropriate to address the drug abuse problem first — others may prove to be more pressing.

To do a thorough assessment, the clinician must consider all of the following in their proper context:

— The adolescent's development, how is he or she doing now, and the relationship to the presenting problem.

— The family's history, how is it doing now, and the relationship to the presenting problem.

— Past social events and influences, social circumstances now, and the relationship to the presenting problem.

The multiplicity of factors involved in assessing chemical dependency can make the clinician's job a difficult one. Yet, with experience it becomes second nature, and less overwhelming. The essential constant that weaves through the fabric of assessing chemical dependency is that of measuring everything in relationship to the client's total environment and internal experience. If you take your time and consider all the factors presented above, then you will have done your job well.

Chapter 4

Initiating Therapy

Beginning therapy with an adolescent can be quite trying, and especially so with one who has a history of drug abuse. It can be likened to parachuting into enemy territory armed only with your learned, or inherent skills, your charm, a reservoir of energy, and most important of all, your strategy! When it comes to head-to-head combat, the enemy is better equipped, has more experience, and will always win. As a therapist, your only hope for success is to out-maneuver the adolescent and lure him into a cease-fire and eventual armistice. The following chapter will describe how to engage an adolescent in therapy, and subsequent strategies for change. Some of what is presented may challenge previously held beliefs about therapy and counseling. The adolescent demands special skills from the counselor, and flexibility in approach is essential for success. Because many of the methods offered in this chapter are earmarked with my own style, I will speak to you in first person. What you do with a client in a counseling session is exceptionally personal. To adequately describe the process, I can only do so if I can describe my own inner experience as well.

Preparing for the First Session

As I have discussed in workshops and other writings, a counselor is limited by the extent to which he knows himself. So, even before the client arrives, you must ask yourself, "What do I know about myself?" Of course, a complete inventory is not necessary before each counseling session. But, hopefully, you know what you do and do not know about yourself, and the environment you live within. We all carry a certain set of presuppositions into every situation, and especially the therapeutic relationship. The adolescent client knows more about himself and his environment than you ever will, although the adolescent may not be able to understand all that he knows or, even less, how to adjust to that knowledge.

Before the client and/or his family arrives, another question we must ask ourselves is, "What is my model?" Do you know what you are going to do? What are your options? What "stances" or "postures" are you able to assume with adolescents? In other words, what am I looking for in the early going, and how do I want to represent myself to this young person, and to his parents? I may want to show one face to Mom and Dad, and another to their child.

In most every case, I open the session with an acknowledgment of what I do not know. For instance, "What brings you folks here today?" I will ask several "what and how" questions. It is not uncommon that when a counselor has a client referred to her by another agency (i.e., juvenile court, schools, etc.) she may have received considerable data on the person prior to his arrival. Even if I have read some of the information, or was bombarded over the phone by the referring agent, I try to appear ignorant. I am entering the adolescent's territory, and I must observe the territorial boundaries. I must accept them as they present themselves to me, at least initially. I may confront them later with the inconsistencies of earlier statements.

The family and the individual are presenting me with a gift, and I cannot "spit" on it and reject it. I may want to change the gift later, but initially I am obliged to accept it.

Adolescents with drug abuse problems arrive for counseling in a variety of ways. Most often, they arrive under duress. They have been threatened, coerced, bribed and even lied to about where they are going. Also, the drug-abusing adolescent, if he/she knows whom they are going to see, will be quite defensive and elusive. Strategically, I must join new clients wherever there is an opening. Frequently I will join them on the very issue of how they got to my office. "Whose idea was it for you to come here today?", is a typical opener. "What did you expect from coming here today?", is a common following opener. I do not believe it is advisable to tackle an adolescent head on. The individual may be experimenting, may be abusing, or may be chemically dependent. As was stressed in the previous chapter, there is no way to know for sure about an adolescent within the first interview.

When an adolescent first arrives in my office, I generally anticipate anxiety on his part. Even if the young person acts cool and relaxed, that may not be his inner experience. However, occasionally I will run across a counseling veteran who has been dragged by his parents to numerous counselors. Usually these adolescents view counseling as a game, where they have won more than they have lost. In this case, the adolescent may feel confident enough to try to take charge and confront me.

When an adolescent attempts to dominate me, I must do whatever I can to sidestep this trap. I do not want to resort to some kind of counter power play if I can avoid it. Also, I do not want the adolescent to view me as a pushover, and feel he has successfully conned another counselor. Tactically, at this point, I want to do the unexpected. I may say, "You're really good at this aren't you. You seem to be in control of yourself and know what you want to accomplish here. I can tell you've done this before. This is really great, I love a challenge, and you seem like you would be fun to work with. Is that what you do at home when your parents try to confront you about your drug use?" It is important that there be sincere enthusiasm in my voice. Sarcasm will not work. The message I want to send is that I know what they are up to, it is okay, and I will not judge them. But, I will not be overpowered either. My integrity is unshakable and I am comfortable with myself.

On rare occasions, the adolescent will vow to his parents that he will not talk to the counselor. And, in fact, they do not say a word. Usually I am not swayed by these passionate and dramatic declarations of silence. I usually can get most adolescents to talk to me eventually. But, then there was Wanda. She made her vow and kept it! I tried every ploy I knew to get just one word out of her. Nothing worked. Then I made a tactical mistake. I said, "Okay I can wait, when you feel ready to talk, then I'll be ready." I waited and waited and she never said a word. I had lost, but also learned from the experience.

Although Wanda was verbally silent, she was still communicating. Her body said a great deal to me, and I overlooked this. She looked at the floor the entire hour, kept her arms folded and tapped her feet constantly. Not exactly the nonverbal cues of a relaxed person, I would say. But, I focused all my energy on approaching her verbally. The harder I tried, the more powerful she became. My silence was the final acknowledgment that I had failed.

How should I have dealt with Wanda?

First, I should have never stopped talking. She was in the room and, as far as I knew, had perfect hearing. If she would not talk, then I could have continued to talk, knowing that she heard every word. I could have talked about anything, but especially about her nonverbal behavior. I could have utilized some Ericksonian hypnotic methods to intervene on the situation (Ritterman, 1984). I could have said, "Very good, looking at the floor may be comfortable for you, and you may want to keep it up. The more you keep your arms folded, the more relaxed you may feel. And the more you tap your foot, the less anxious you may feel." I would continue to talk to Wanda this way, and encourage her to continue doing what she was doing. I would point out to Wanda that she was responding in a way just right for her, given her present circumstances. I am reminded of a story a friend tells about when he worked at a psychiatric hospital. On one of the units, there was a patient who would periodically become catatonic. It was not uncommon for this patient to do this in the hallway. Some people would stop and talk to him and try to talk him out of his catatonic state. Others would just ignore him and walk around him. When my friend encountered this patient doing his "thing" in the hallway, he walked up to him and assumed the same posture right next to him. My friend learned two things from this experience. First, it takes a tremendous amount of energy to maintain the same posture for an extended length of time. And second, after about half an hour, the patient turned to him and said, "What are you doing you s.o.b.," and walked away. My friend's intervention was quite powerful, but was not a direct effort to control the patient.

In the early stages of counseling, adolescents and their parents tend to do a lot of blaming in the session. It is impossible to avoid this, and the counselor needs to be prepared to listen to some of it.

Everyone needs to feel like he was at least allowed to voice his side of things. If one person is going to do some blaming, then I believe that everyone should have a turn.

Once the blaming has finished, or I have redirected things, it is time to get on with the task at hand. In the previous chapter, I outlined a procedure for doing an assessment. I will not repeat that here. The next section will be devoted to a summary of the therapy with three of the cases covered in the last chapter. These case summaries will outline significant events and developments in the cases of Sharon, Billy and Richard.

Getting Down To Business

First: Assault on the Iron Maiden

After considering the assessment data presented in the previous chapter, it was time to decide how to proceed with Sharon therapeutically. It is my practice to start with the least restrictive therapy modality first. Occasionaly, I will be presented with an adolescent whom I can clearly see needs to go to the hospital immediately, without passing go. In Sharon's case, I felt it was worth trying counseling on an outpatient basis first. Later in therapy, I determined this was a mistake. But first, the outpatient efforts will be reviewed.

As described in Chapter Three, Sharon's appearance was harsh and cold to the outside observer. Yet, she also possessed an ability to be coy and sweet — skills she had learned for dealing with Dad and most of the men she came in contact. In our first session alone, Sharon was clearly trying her best to be unoffensive. In this situation, drug-abusing adolescents are confident in their abilities to divert adults away from their drug use.

Therapist: Sharon, obviously some people feel that you have a problem with drugs. Why would they think that?
Sharon: I don't know.
Therapist: Do you think they are making it up?
Sharon: No.

Obviously, this little interchange was not very productive, but it is typical of the posture many adolescents take when confronted by a counselor. Tell the counselor as little as possible, and maybe he will go away. This strategy has worked with parents and other adults before, so stick with something that works is the adolescent's belief.

Therapist: Well, tell me about the first time you got high. Was it fun? Who were you with?

It seems best at this point to just move on into a frank discussion about Sharon's drug use. Avoid the isssue of having to admit to a "problem," and allow Sharon to tell what she knows. Usually adolescents are not sophisticated enough to resist this invitation.

Sharon: Yeah, sure it was fun. It was after school over at Shelley's house. She had some marijuana and we smoked two joints. It was no big deal, and we just wanted to see what it was like.

Therapist: Did you and Shelley continue to get high together then?

Sharon: Yeah. We would usually go over after school, and sometimes Julie and Amy would come too.

Therapist: Would you just talk and laugh and have a good time?

Sharon: Yeah. We had lots of fun. It seemed we could relax and be ourselves for once, without worrying about someone coming down on us.

Therapist: You did this a lot, didn't you?

Sharon: Almost every day. And then we would meet before school and get high. Julie and Amy didn't like that, but Shelley did.

Up to this point Sharon's enthusiasm had built to where she was proudly telling about her experiences. I was attempting to make no judgments about her story, but simply facilitating the telling of it. During this short interchange, I learned a great deal about Sharon — drugs created a feeling which she was starving for, and she had a strong attraction to them immediately.

Drug-abusing adolescents generally are not just protecting their own use, but may be protecting others as well. They are often protecting members of their family. In Sharon's family, there was a conflict between Mom and Dad, and it was about Dad's drinking. It was tense at home, and Sharon's parents were continually fighting, but mostly about her. Rarely did Mom and Dad discuss Dad's drinking. Sharon was quite effective in diverting attention away from Dad, and onto herself. There was an unspoken alliance between Sharon and her father. This was a partial explanation for Sharon to seek a source of relief. Getting high with Shelley became just the ticket. Actually, Shelley had problems at home too, and so a coalition formed between the two of them. This coalition became the source of numerous family arguments.

Mom: Sharon, we know you have been sneaking out to be with Shelley at night, and this has got to stop. That girl is a bad influence on you. I know she has troubles at home, but you can't let her troubles become yours.

Sharon: You don't know anything about Shelley! It's not any of your business who my friends are. It's my life, and I can do whatever I want with it. Shelley is my friend, and I won't dump her for you, or anybody. (Sharon glares around the room, including everyone in her ultimatum).

Therapist: Dad, what do you have to say about this?

Dad: Well, I know Shelley has problems, but what teenager doesn't.

Dad's reponse was weak and minimally supportive of Mom. It seemed that Dad was respecting Sharon's stated desire for non-interference with her friends. This then made it difficult for Sharon's mother to enforce her earlier statement about Shelley.

Mom: Phil, you know we can't let Sharon run loose at night with that girl!

Sharon: That girl! There is nothing wrong with Shelley! If there is anything wrong with anybody, it's you! You think you're so much better than anybody else!

Dad: Now Sharon, I won't have you talking to your mother that way. Just calm down.

Therapist: Phil, it seems that the issue here is whether you agree with your wife. It appears that Sharon has more power than you in this argument over Shelley.

Mom: Yeah, and she won't listen to me either. She thinks she runs the household.

Sharon: I don't run anything around here. I never get anything I want. (Shouting at Mom) You're always on my back about something.

The interchange above was typical for Sharon's family. Sharon got off the hook and Mom and Dad were left to argue with each other. This led to an excuse for Dad to drink, and then all interaction would stop. Dad would withdraw, Sharon would isolate herself, leaving only Mom and little sister Kelly to interact with each other.

This family system was in a very delicate balance which could easily be upset by a bold and dramatic intervention. My concerns were with the family's ability to cope with a direct confrontation of Dad's drinking, and the fundamental marital dysfunction. Furthermore, Sharon's drug use seemed to be accelerated by the counseling. I was a threat to the system, and might break up the alliance between Sharon, her dad and Shelley. Sharon's behavior became more outrageous, forcing the attention to remain upon her. If Sharon were to allow Mom and Dad to cooperate together, then that might mean the end of her drug use. On the other hand, Dad's drinking was being threatened by counseling, and he was feeling the pressure to support his wife. Phil was afraid the subject of his drinking would come up. However, Sharon had been successful in keeping the family away from this issue.

Strategically, it was time for a dramatic move. I chose to see the parents alone and tell them that Sharon would not get better unless we admitted her to an adolescent chemical dependency unit. I told them that I felt Sharon's life was at stake, and we could no longer afford to take risks with it. At first, Sharon's parents were skeptical. This move seemed drastic and scary. I assured them that it was necessary. Sharon's drug use had evolved to a point where I did not believe she could quit on her own. I explained what would happen in treatment, how long it would last, and aswered all the questions Sharon's parents had about this decision. I suspected Phil would view this development as an opportunity to get the heat off of him, since Sharon would be the one in the hospital. He did not realize what would come later, and how he would be confronted about his drinking.

When a counselor informs the parents that their child must be hospitalized for chemical dependency, it is an extrememly sensitive moment. Most parents view this development as catastrophic and are dependent upon the counselor to support and guide them. It is typical to find parents feeling guilty, that they somehow caused their child's condition. "If we had just been better parents, this would not be happening." This is a common response, as well as, "If you had just spent more time with her, we wouldn't have to send her away now." Unfortunately, some parents will resort to blaming each other and the counselor must interrupt this and set everyone straight. Even other children in the family may feel like they somehow contributed to their sibling going to the hospital.

The counselor must instruct everyone that now is a time to support each other. The hospitalization is necessary, and the family can only help the child if they accept it and suspend any blaming.

In Sharon's case, the family was too confused and disorganized to effectively deal with her. Also, Sharon's behavior and drug use was out of control, and she would not acknowledge her dependency. The hospital environment could provide a firm structure for the entire family to operate within (Kolb, et. al., 1982). The hospital staff could also bring the drug use under control and direct the family in how to deal with Sharon's dependency. It is generally best to treat the most "salient" problem first (Weissman, 1980). In this case, Sharon's deterioration was the most pressing problem, and needed immediate containment. If an adolescent's internal problems are too severe, he/she may be unable to internalize the interactional process of family therapy.

Once I had decided to recommend hospitalization for Sharon, I knew I had to proceed carefully. I felt confident I could convince Sharon's parents to put her in the hospital. But, I also knew that if I presented this idea too early, Sharon might run away. With our society's sensitivity about runaways and missing children, I knew I did not want to precipitate a more serious problem.

I met with the parents alone and enlisted their support on the issue of hospitalization. Then I called the hospital to make sure there was an empty bed for Sharon, and there was. At this point I gave the phone to Sharon's father so he could pass on the necessary information regarding insurance and basic demographics on

Sharon and the family.

The next step was to inform Sharon that she was going to the hospital and then simply take her there, immediately. This, of course, was met with intense resistance.

Sharon: No way! You're not taking me to that place. That's for burnouts, and I'm not one of those. I won't go!

Father: Sharon you have to go. Your mother and I can no longer handle you at home. This is not something you have a choice in. We have probably let you have your way on too may things. But this is something we have decided, and we are going to take you now.

Sharon: Daddy, please don't take me there! I promise I'll be good. I'll do whatever you say, just let me stay home. It's my home too. You can't just throw me out.

Father: We are not throwing you out Sharon, you will return home after you are through with treatment. Your mother and I will be waiting for you. This is the best thing for you right now.

Sharon: I thought I could trust you (to father), now I can't even trust my own parents. This isn't fair. If anybody should go to the hospital it should be you! You're the one that drinks himself to sleep every night in front of the TV. You're just a. . .

Father: That's enough Sharon. You're going and that is all there is to it.

Now Dad was angry and threatened. On the power of his anger, he then whisked Sharon off to the hospital. Sharon was about to betray him as he had just betrayed her, and he would have nothing to do with it. In a sense, he put her in the hospital to shut her up. At this point, my only concern was that Sharon got to the hospital. We could deal with betrayal issues later.

Once Sharon was in the hospital, she attempted to stonewall her way back out. She would not communicate, other than to answer direct questions and in one or two word answers. Sharon's belief was that if she did not cooperate, the staff would tire of her and let her go home. However, the staff were used to this tactic and simply waited. For a week, Sharon was allowed to remain in her silence. On the eighth day, Sharon realized that stonewalling was not working, and so she changed her tactic. She became more cooperative, and began to mimic what she had seen some of the other kids do, especially those who were close to being released.

Suddenly, Sharon confessed to using drugs, to being chemically dependent, and to feeling "real" remorse for all she had done. "I know I'm a drug addict, and I always will be one. I won't ever use drugs again. I've learned my lesson. I'm glad my parents brought me here, because I can see now that I need help. But honestly, I feel much better now. I think I'm ready to go home."

The staff were unimpressed and seemed almost uninterested in these admissions on Sharon's part. Even the other kids on the unit were not impressed, and almost ignored Sharon. Sharon could not believe the lack of response to her best efforts. It made her furious, and she began to rage at the staff and other patients, and call them the worst names she could think of. "All you people here are idiots and should be put in jail for keeping people against their will. This is the dumbest place I've ever seen, and I want out of here now. You have no right to keep me here," Sharon shouted.

For the first time, the staff and other kids seemed to take a real interest in what Sharon had to say. To them it was the first demonstration of real feeling since Sharon had arrived on the unit. Sharon's counselor said to her, "Finally I am hearing something genuine from you. It's about time you got in touch with your anger and your fear. Did you know you were afraid?"

"Why should I be afraid of you, you're all a bunch of jerks anyway." Sharon's voice was full of self righteousness.

"It's not us you're afraid of, it's Sharon that scares you," said her counselor.

"You're nuts, why should I be afraid of myself?" Sharon reported sharply.

At this point, therapy could begin with Sharon. She was desperate and coming face-to-face with her deepest fears. The staff knew this and would not allow Sharon off the hook, but were also patient with her. At this point, it was time to start setting goals for Sharon's treatment. It would have been useless to try and set goals in Sharon's first week of treatment. The staff had to address the following questions first:

1. What needs to change in this adolescent?
2. What needs to change in her circumstance?
3. What needs to change in her environment?
4. What else do the staff need to know?
5. Is it clear who will be doing what? (Steinberg, 1983)

In Sharon's case, there were several behaviors and attitudes that needed to change (question #1). As is typical of chemically dependent adolescents, Sharon was angry and hostile. Sharon needed to express these feelings, and understand them, and then learn how to appropriately express her anger. Egan points out how many drug-abusing adolescents are angry, have a fear of failure, tend to sensationalize, have difficulty learning from others, deny their own problems, but also desire to have a relationship (Egan, 1980). Sharon possessed all of these characteristics. All of these things needed to change if Sharon was to develop and stay straight. Sharon's dependency was preventing her from completing those developmental tasks relevant to her age. One purpose of treatment was to free Sharon from those behavioral and attitudinal blocks to normal development.

Sharon was also experiencing low self-esteem. Sharon's only success was her effectiveness at getting high when she wanted and covering it up. These accomplishments did not bring her much self satisfaction. Sharon needed to begin fulfulling some basic tasks, and then experiencing rewards for their completion. Sharon needed to be given responsibilities on the unit.

Chemically dependent kids tend to avoid non-dependent kids who might not approve of their lifestyle. Dependent kids tend to hang out with others like themselves who rely on drugs to deal with stress. This results in an inablity to solve problems on their own, and so they rarely experience any sense of accomplishment (Reardon, et.al., 1983).

What needs to change in Sharon's circumstance is that she must accept that she cannot use any drugs or alcohol. Sharon will need to adopt the principles of Alcoholics Anonymous. Due to her dependency upon drugs, Sharon is subject to a unique status. She must commit herself, on a daily basis, to not use any drugs that day. This commitment will require a major re-organization of her self identity. Sharon's sobriety must become her number one priority.

What needs to change in Sharon's environment refers to the way she interacts with others, particularly her family. Also in this category is how Sharon interacts with her school environment, social environment and her treatment environment. At this point, Sharon's family was brought into therapy. Sharon's parents were first exposed to a thorough education about chemical dependency and their roles as family members of a dependent person.

After the education process, it became necessary to confront Sharon's father about his drinking. He was not surprised. Sharon's father saw it coming as he sat through the educational sessions. There was some initial resistance to the confrontation, but eventually he accepted he had a problem. Intervention was easier, since Sharon was out of the picture and did not serve as a distraction. Sharon's father entered an out-patient alcoholism counseling program and began attending AA meetings.

As Sharon proceeded through treatment, the staff administered some psychological tests to determine if there was anything else they may have overlooked. This was in response to question number 4. Clinicians need to be careful when administering psychological tests to adolescents, especially the MMPI (Minnesota Multiphasic Personality Inventory). Research has shown that it is not advisable to administer adult scales of the MMPI to adolescents (Klunge, et. al., 1978). Adolescents taking the adult scales tend to appear more pathological than they really are. Or, normal adolescents may appear as pathological on the adult scales. Chemically dependent kids score nearly the same as non-dependent kids on the adolescent scales of the MMPI. Most adolescents tend to have the same elevated scales on the MMPI, but the drug-abusing population seems to score slightly higher on those scales. Interpreting the standard MMPI scales as diagnostic of chemical dependency is cautioned when applied to adolescents. However, the MacAndrew Alcoholism scale does seem to have some validity when diagnosing adolescents. In other words, an elevated standard MMPI scale does not necessarily indicate the presence of pathology, nor chemical dependency.

Finally, it becomes necessary to determine who on the staff will be responsible for what therapeutic strategies (question #5). Sharons' primary counselor obviously is responsible for the day-to-day course of therapy. But, as Sharon's family became involved in therapy, a family therapist was added. It is generally best to allow the family therapist to take charge of the continued therapy of the patient and their family. As the parents become more involved, issues of family reunification may surface. With the primary counselor's cooperation, the family therapist takes charge of coordinating Sharon's reintegration back into her family. To do this effectively, the parents must make frequent visits to the hospital to be in on therapeutic interventions with Sharon (Ellis, 1984).

With the treatment staff coordinating and structuring the family's get-together, Sharon's recovery was quick. Separating Sharon from her family allowed Sharon to focus upon her own problems, and for her family to come to an understanding of theirs. Without the interference of drugs and alcohol, Sharon's family was able to begin solving its own problems.

Billy: A Brief Intervention

As mentioned in the previous chapter, Billy's use of alcohol seemed to be abusive in nature, but not dependent. As a therapist, I felt there was good potential to resolve Billy's problems quickly, with the cooperation of his parents. In this family, the mother and father were simply not functioning effectively, and the children had too much control. Billy was the worst example of a child exceeding his limits within the family hierarchy. Also, Billy's drinking was dangerous and had to stop immediately.

Family therapy was indicated in Billy's case. Billy had not deteriorated like Sharon, and there was no apparent reason why the parents could not get the situation under control. It was essential that we hit this drinking problem "hard" and quickly. I instructed the parents to forbid Billy to drink ever again, as long as he lived in their house. At first there was some confusion about this task.

Therapist: Do you (to the parents) feel it is okay for Billy to drink alcohol?
Mother: Absolutely not! I know kids his age drink and there is a lot of pressure to do it, but I do not want Billy to. It scares me when he is driving our car to think he might be drunk.
Therapist: Dad, what do you think?
Father: Well, I suppose if he would just learn to handle it and not let himself get drunk. I know kids are going to drink.

If Billy were a different kid, maybe Dad's belief would be reasonable. But, this is a father who does not really know his son, nor his capabilities. The mother is more in touch with her son's behavioral capacities. Strategically, it is best to maneuver the father into a more realistic attitude about his son. It is important not to violate Billy's confidentiality, yet still educate his father about what happens when teenagers abuse alcohol.

Therapist: (To the parents) It seems to me that it might be helpful for both of you to learn more about adolescents and alcohol abuse. I know of an alcohol education class which I would like you to attend for one week. Also, I would like you to speak with the Community Liaison Officer at the Police Department. He can tell you about the numbers of arrests in a given week related to teenage drinking. I want you to do this before our next appointment. Billy, I have some things I want you to do also, but I want your parents to do their homework first.

Billy's parents agreed to do the assignment, and we arranged another appoinment in about 10 days. As the family prepared to leave, Billy appeared nervous and not as cocky as when he first came in. Although Billy's parents had not actually done anything yet, there was a strong implication that things might change. I predicted Billy would escalate the conflicts at home to try and assert his control, but would probably not come home drunk in the next ten days.

After 10 days the family returned

Therapist: (To the parents) Well, did you do your assignments?

Mother: Yes we did, and we found it very enlightening (she nods and smiles a sly smile towards her husband).

Therapist: Bob, did you learn anything interesting?

Father: Yes, I did. I didn't realize how much trouble kids get into in this town due to drinking. The police statistics were sobering. I couldn't believe how many kids they detain on just one Friday night. Also, all the disturbance calls due to kids drinking and raising hell (he shakes his head as if in disbelief).

Billy: Oh, the cops are just a bunch of red-necked hardasses! They bust people for doing nothing at all (he interrupts excitedly).

Father: Well I wonder if maybe you're one of those people the police were talking about. In the class, we learned about that attitude, the one you're showing us now.

Billy has incriminated himself and his father can see the light. Fortunately, I did not have to violate what Billy told me in confidence. Billy's father can see for himself now that his son is running the risk of getting into serious trouble and it cannot be ignored.

Therapist: Well, that is interesting. It sounds like both of you (to parents) may have come to some new conclusions about Billy's drinking. (At this point, I want to be sure to talk to both parents as if they are already unified in a decision. And I want to defer to Bob so I can reinforce his position as head of the household.) What have you decided Bob?

Father: (Looking at his wife and back to me.) We have decided that under no circumstance is Billy to drink alcohol of any kind. Obviously he cannot handle alcohol and we don't want him getting into the kind of trouble some kids do.

Therapist: Well, I'm glad to see you're in agreement on this issue, because this will make the rest of our work together easier. (I reinforce them again for being in agreement.)

Mother: Yes, I think it was very enlightening for Bob to attend that class, and the officer was very helpful. The officer was surprised at our interest. He said few parents ever call him to ask about teenage drinking on their own.

Therapist: Well, very good. Now, Billy, I have some assignments for you, too. But before I get into that I need to know if you will back me up (I look at the parents again)?

Parents: Of course! (They both nod in agreement to my request for support.)

Billy: Listen, I've done alright already. I didn't come home drunk last week and I didn't get into any trouble at school.

Mother: Yes, but you were perfectly awful at home. You fought with me about everything, hit you're little brother and screamed at your sister. That has got to stop.

Father: Yes, we saw the very behavior they talked about in the class. It could very well be related to drinking. But, either way, you will have to behave better at home.

Therapist: This is where I need your help. There need to be consequences for Billy's unacceptable behavior, and you have to be consistent about enforcing them. I believe Billy will need to understand more about the dangerous consequences of drinking, and he may need some help in giving it up. Billy, I want you to attend an alcohol education class for teenagers starting next week. And, I want you to go to one AA meeting a week for the next six weeks. (Turning to the parents) And, if he doesn't do it, what will be the consequences?

After some discussion Billy's parents agreed that if he did not do the assignment he could not use the car, nor leave the house for a week. Billy protested these consequences, but for once, his parents did not waver and his complaining was in vain. Similar consequences were arranged for any future violent outbursts at home.

I continued to see Billy and his family for several more weeks but at a decreasing frequency. It was important to reinforce the parents to continue to work together as a team. Billy followed his assignment at first, but one week he did not go to his AA meeting, and another time he missed his alcohol class. On both occasions, Billy's parents followed through with the consequences. Gradually, Billy's behavior improved at home, as he discovered he could not get around the limits set in therapy.

In subsequent sessions, Billy's parents discussed his self concept with him and pointed out other virtues he possessed. Billy seemed to brighten up when his father told him how he envied his ability to communicate verbally. "I've always been quiet and shy. Sometimes I feel I could have gone farther in my career if I could just communicate better. But, you seem to be able to get others attention so naturally. People seem to be drawn to you, Billy, and you like it. I've always felt uncomfortable when I thought people were noticing me. I wish I had some of your charm."

I followed the family for two more months, just to monitor their progress. Steadily, I could see improvements in Billy's attitudes. But, more importantly, I could see the parents cooperating better, and supporting each other in most decisions. After three months in therapy, there were no more drinking episodes. Billy's grades improved and a friend even got him to join the debate team at school. Six months after I first saw Billy, he dropped by my office with his girlfriend and his new sports car. He had a part-time job and was helping to pay for the car.

Residential Treatment with Richard

Richard arrived at the hospital in bad shape. He spent three days in detox with shakes, severe anxiety followed by depression and a withdrawal into himself. Once the staff felt Richard was over the initial physical symptoms, he was placed on the adolescent treatment unit for further observation. The staff did not expect a great deal from Richard in his first few days of treatment.

Richard's psychological testing indicated that he was depressed, had some thought disturbances and possessed poor reality-checking abilities. Richard had difficulty matching the appropriate feelings to specific situations presented during the testing period. Richard still lived in his fantasy world, and felt very uncomfortable without his drugs.

After a couple of days on the unit, Richard attempted to get close to one of the more vulnerable and seductive female patients. Richard would meet with the girl away from the other patients, and was caught in her room one night by the nurse. Richard was restricted from any further contact with the girl. Richard had no way to fulfull his need for pleasure, and was progressively growing more frustrated.

The psychological testing indicated that Richard might also be at risk for suicide, and so the staff watched him carefully. When confronted directly about suicide, Richard denied it, but his flat affect seemed to indicate otherwise.

Richard's mother was allowed to visit him only for a few hours on Sunday afternoons. In the meantime, she was busy monitoring her husband's deteriorating health at another hospital across town. Richard seemed more interested in getting out of the hospital, than in his adoptive father's condition. Then it dawned on Richard to appeal to the staff's sympathies and let him out, due to his father's illness. The staff refused to release Richard so he could see his father, and so he withdrew even further.

In group counseling, Richard began to offer bits and pieces of his drug use history. Richard told stories comparable to the other patient's, but he was only scratching the surface of the full extent of his drug use. As the days passed, Richard began to tell more and more about his drug use, his stealing and even all the sex he had with girls. Richard even confessed to having oral sex with one of the pushers who supplied him with drugs. "I would do it to him when I didn't have enough money to buy dope." Richard shared each sordid story with the same lack of feeling, as if it had happened to someone else. However, Richard was always careful to avoid telling anything about what went on between he and his niece.

In group, some of the girls would tell of being raped by their fathers, even attacked by uncles and sometimes their own brothers. When these subjects would come up, Richard would become very uncomfortable. Usually quiet in group, Richard would lean back in his chair and even move out of the circle when incest was mentioned. This was the time when Richard would usually request to get up and go to the bathroom, even though he knew it was not allowed during group.

At first, the counselors paid no attention to Richard's behavior when incest was mentioned in group. But, it so happened that Richard fell into a group where several girls reported having had incestual experiences. For several days in a row, the subject was discussed in group. Richard's anxiety was reaching uncontrollable limits and it was all he could do to conceal it.

Finally, it became apparent that something was troubling Richard, because he was becoming progressively more agitated. Once, Richard blurted out in group, "Do we have to talk about this again, it's all we seem to talk about. I'm tired of it!" This was quite uncharacteristic of Richard to become so emotional. Everyone in group turned and looked at him in stunned silence.

Counselor: This subject seems to make you uncomfortable, Richard. Has something similar happened to you? (The counselor was assuming Richard had been the victim of incest, too.)

Richard: No! Nobody ever done nothin' like that to me. It's just that it's so disgusting, and I get tired of hearing about it. It seems like all them girls want is for us to feel sorry for them. That's all.

Counselor: You sound angry at the girls because they were the victims of incest.

Richard: Victims! (Richard's voice becomes shrill, his face gets red and his knuckles go white from clenching his fists so tight.) You know how girls are. They probably asked for it, anyway. Girls are always wanting sex. Anybody can tell that.

Julie: You're nuts! I never asked my dad to have sex with me. He's sick and I was just a kid and couldn't stop him. Why would I want to have sex with my dad, anyway? You're just weird!

Richard: Shut up you bitch!

Counselor: Calm down, Richard, or I'll put you on restriction.

Richard: Go ahead, see what I care. You're all a bunch of assholes here anyway. I don't belong here. Just leave me alone.

Counselor: No one was bothering you Richard, you started this. And now you're going to get the consequences for it. You're restricted to your room for the rest of the day.

John: Hey Richard, what are you getting so hot about anyway. Did you screw your sister or something (one of the patient said sarcastically)?

At this point, Richard could take no more. He came out of his chair and jumped on John before the counselor could get between them. The other adolescents sat riveted to their seats. They did not believe Richard was capable of this type of behavior, and could only watch as the counselor pulled Richard off of John. John was okay, but Richard was out of control. The veins in Richard's neck and head were sticking out, his teeth were clenched tightly, sweat was flowing out of every pore. The counselor continued to hold Richard as tight as he could while Richard struggled to get free. Then came the tears, and then the sobs which shook both Richard and the counselor, they were so heavy. Richard went limp in the counselor's arms and they both slumped to the floor with the counselor still holding Richard as he continued to sob.

"I'm sorry, I'm sorry. I didn't mean to, I didn't mean to." The words came out in between the sobs as Richard now clutched tightly to the counselor.

"I couldn't stop myself. I didn't want to do it, but I thought she wanted me too. I'm sorry, please, I'm sorry."

Who are you talking about Richard," the counselor asked gently.

"Jennifer, Jennifer, my little niece. I'm sorry, I didn't mean it."

The counselor continued to hold Richard as he sobbed. Then sobbing began to subside a little. The rest of the group had been on the edge of their chairs, but as they saw Richard begin to calm down they could relax some. At this point, Julie timidly moved over to Richard and the counselor and carefully put her arms around Richard also. Julie had tears in her eyes too as she held on to Richard tighter.

Eventually, Richard calmed down enough so that he could talk again. Then Richard told the whole story of what happened between he and his niece, and everyone listened quietly. A tremendous burden had been lifted from Richard's shoulders. The rest of the group helped and supported Richard through the experience. From this point, Richard's treatment took a 180 degree turn for the better.

In the following days, Richard came to understand that he was addicted to drugs and sex as well. Richard realized that his life was out of control, that sex and drugs were in the driver's seat. Richard's affect was still somewhat flat, but the emotional outburst over the incest left him nearly defenseless and open to therapy. Richard began to adopt the principles of AA and experience a new sense of belonging to a group which he had never felt before.

Richard was vulnerable to what ever the staff told him, and he would accept any feedback. Somehow, Richard knew he was incomplete and needed help to develop to a point matching his chronological age. The staff were concerned that Richard may be simply echoing what he heard, and was not actually integrating it. Psychologically, Richard was only about 12 years old. It is fairly common knowledge that 12 year olds rarely benefit from inpatient treatment. This age group is developmentally incapable of integrating the sophisticated concepts presented in treatment. Was Richard simply acting like he thought he was supposed to? Richard's motivation seemed sincere, he knew he needed help and was becoming quite dependent upon the staff and patients.

Then something happened that intensified the staff's concerns. Richard's father died from a massive heart attack. Richard had been doing well up to that point, even though some suspected the depth of his understanding. Richard's reaction to his father's death was one of a blank stare. Again, he was unable to match the appropriate feeling with the situation. It seemed like he should feel sad, but he felt nothing. Richard knew enough to really suspect something was wrong with him. Everyone around Richard seemed more upset by his father's death than he did! "I know I should feel something, but I just don't. I don't even know if I loved my father. How do you know if you love someone?", Richard shared impassionately with his counselor.

At this point, the staff knew Richard's recovery would be slow, and he would need ongoing therapy for many months. The time for Richard's release from treatment was drawing near. It was decided to move Richard to an adolescent halfway house for three months. Richard accepted he was chemically and sexually dependent and talked the talk, but everyone was still concerned that he might fail if not closely supervised.

Richard's mother was not handling her grief well. She was intensely angry over her loss, but was unable to identify her anger. Richard's mother had suffered several blows in a short amount of time. Her son's arrest, learning he was chemically dependent, and then learning that he had had sex with her granddaughter, and finally her husband's death, was all just too much. Her coping mechanisms were overloaded, and she withdrew into her home. Richard's mother had attended a week of family treatment at the hospital, but she did not really benefit from it. Her attention was divided between her son and her husband. She never really accepted Richard's dependencies. She was overwhelmed by guilt that she could have overlooked Richard's drug use for so long. She was especially guilt-ridden over not realizing what was going on between Richard and her granddaughter.

Richard's stay at the halfway house was uneventful. Richard went to group counseling, AA meetings and to school at the hospital each day. The halfway house personnel were used to more advanced patients, and felt Richard was not living up to their expectations. This was when Richard was referred to me.

Obviously, there was much work left to be done when Richard arrived at my office. I will continue with Richard's case in Chapter Seven, where I will discuss treatment follow-up.

Outpatient vs Inpatient Treatment

In the cases presented in this chapter, decisions regarding treatment modalities were made according to differing situations and personal capacities. The practitioner needs to possess a set of criteria for determining the best treatment modality for an adolescent. Some of these criteria were mentioned in Chapter Three. In addition to differing criteria, there are also different treatment goals relevant to outpatient vs inpatient threatment.

When setting therapeutic goals with an adolescent, the counselor must give careful consideration to : (1) the age and abilities of the adolescent; (2) the capabilities of the adolescent's family to cooperate in therapy; (3) what is age appropriate behavior for a given adolescent's level of development; (4) what level of understanding is a given adolescent capable of; and finally, (5) what are the purposes of inpatient and outpatient treatment?

A counselor well versed in adolescent development and family dynamics should be able to adequately address questions 1 through 4. The final section will discuss treatment goals appropriate for inpatient and outpatient settings.

Outpatient Goals

The counselor working in an outpatient setting must first assess how appropriate it is for a given adolescent to be seen in that setting. If the counselor determines that inpatient treatment is inappropriate, then he must work with the adolescent and the family to identify specific goals. The following is a list of possible goals which a counselor may wish to address with his client(s).

1. Abstinence from all mood-altering substances.
2. Attend all scheduled counseling sessions.
3. Attend school regularly.
4. Maintain minimally acceptable grades in school.
5. Obey all appointed curfews.
6. Support each other in the enforcement of any of the rules (for parents).

It may take a considerable amount of negotiating and arguing before an agreement can be reached about any, or all, of the above rules. Yet, if the family and the individual adolescent still have the capacity to solve problems, then achieving these goals is not unrealistic. Obviously, other goals may be added to the list, such as attending AA meetings, controlling one's temper, etc. Also, the adolescent and his parents must agree on specific consequences if any of the goals are not achieved. Often, there may not exist any clearly defined decision-making process within the family. This may become one of the most important goals of therapy — to establish a way to make decisions about the children, and to stick to those decisions.

Finally, the counselor may have specific therapeutic goals in mind for her adolescent client. She may want to help the adolescent learn to identify his feelings and to express them in more appropriate ways. Drug abusing kids often have difficulties expressing anger, and often act it out, rather than talk it out. Counseling can become a safe arena within which to discuss these difficult issues. The overall purpose of outpatient counseling is to change inappropriate and unacceptable behavior within the individual, and the family as well.

Inpatient Goals

Counselors working in residential treatment facility are generally more concerned with issues of containment. The hospital provides a place to contain problems, and then to create a climate within which change can begin to occur. The adolescent placed in such a facility is there because he could not be successful in an outpatient program. Also, the adolescent and/or his family was unable to function adequately individually, or together, to solve their own problems. Finally, the adolescent in a hospital is there because his drug use was out of control, and he had become unmanageable. These facts cause counselors to address a different set of goals from those mentioned above. However, there may be some overlap. The fundamental purpose is to contain the adolescent.

Some goals which would be appropriate for inpatient treatment would be as follows:

1. Abstinence from any mood-altering substances.
2. No violent behavior.
3. Understand chemical dependency as a disease.
4. Do a complete history of one's drug use.
5. Begin to identify one's feelings (i.e., mad, sad, glad, hurt, scared and ashamed).

6. Respect the rights of others.
7. Accept that you are powerless over drugs, and that your life has become unmanageable because of this (1st step of AA).
8. Do an honest inventory of your faults and how you may have hurt others in your life (4th step of AA).
9. Accept responsibility for your own recovery.

These goals help the treatment staff to contain the problem and force the adolescent to look at his problem in a new way. The adolescent cannot get away, and must face the consequences of his behavior. Also, the power of the peer group can be brought to bear upon the resistant individual to force a recognition of his dependency. The next two chapters will discuss how to use the group to change behavior, and how to involve the family in both inpatient and outpatient situations.

Chapter 5

Group Therapy

As mentioned in Chapter One, the peer group is a powerful force in the life of any adolescent. The chemically dependent adolescent may be influenced by a smaller segment of peers, but this group is just as influential. Much is said about how peers may pressure a teenager to use drugs. But this pressure is usually highly over-rated. It is the individual's own inner pressure to conform to the group's values which is the strongest force. The adolescents' need to perceive themselves in compliance with the values of their peer group is the stronger drive. As a result, adolescents can be intensely affected by group therapy with others their own age.

This chapter will discuss the power of the group, both positive and negative; the different types of groups appropriate for adolescents; and how to decide when group therapy is appropriate for an individual adolescent.

The Power of the Group

As an age group, adolescents are probably more positively predisposed to the dynamics and purposes of group therapy than any other age group. Adolescents are not so guarded with each other as adults would be, and so can be more candid earlier in therapy. Also, adolescents possess the verbal skills and general intellectual abilities to talk about their feelings, and understand the feelings of others. There is a strong internal motivation to be liked by the group, to impress them, and most important of all, to be accepted. The adolescent identity is fragile and in need of reinforcement. The adult identity is better established, and so there is less need to impress the group, or to even feel a need to join the group.

Although adolescents are predisposed well towards group therapy, this does not necessarily mean they are skilled at doing it. In this regard, adolescents are awkward and need help from a well-trained therapist. Establishing and adhering to some basic ground rules can be difficult for adolescents. In this case, adults tend to follow the rules better than adolescents. Adolescents may be motivated towards group acceptance, but they know relatively little about effective communication. This must be taught, first by the therapist, and then by the group members to each other.

The therapy group is an intense social laboratory where the adolescent can learn and practice more acceptable social skills. Also, this environment provides the chemically dependent youth a chance to interact with peers without the aid of drugs. Most dependent teenagers have had few social experiences with their peers where they were not high. Because the drug-using population tends to accept intoxication, they rarely confront each other about inappropriate behavior. Parents are usually most painfully aware of their dependent child's inability to handle conflicts and confrontation. The dependent person will usually run from a conflict, or try to project the problem onto someone else. In group therapy, there is no escape, but also there are no drugs.

Adolescent group therapy can be quite uneventful, and it may be necessary for the counselor to disrupt this tranquility by being provocative. In this sense, the counselor purposely antagonizes specific group members in order to intensify the level of interaction. In this way, the group members learn what is expected from them. This learning creates a more fluid environment, and the older members can then teach the newer members how to behave. For group therapy to be effective, this member-to-member teaching process must develop. The power of the group cannot develop if the counselor takes the lead all the time. The counselor is advised to try and stir up the interactions, and then back out and allow the group to work on its own. Yet, the counselor must always be ready to intervene again if things get out of control.

All adolescents are concerned about conforming to group values. As the new identity is forming, there is a strong pull towards being a noncomformist. The adolescent wishes to perceive himself as unique and somewhat at odds with adults. The chemically dependent youth is especially disdainful of traditional social values. This group tends to admire their dedication to values and practices which are in defiance of the norm. Many adolescents who are dependent upon drugs may believe they are enlightened, free and above the rest of us.

When these dependent individuals find themselves in a therapy group with other dependent kids, they are uncomfortable. If the group is allowed to talk about the benefits of using drugs, then the tension level will drop. When this occurs, the group will form a shared value system which can be difficult to undermine. These adolescents expect, and rightly so, that the counselor is going to try to impose a more conventional value system upon them. If they can rally the support of the other members, then they can resist this coersive influence by an adult. This is why it is helpful for group leaders to be recovering addicts and relatively young in age. Anything which makes the group leader more credible offers an advantage. Older, non-dependent counselors can be effective in adolescent groups, but they must be exceptionally skillful.

Typical values taught in adolescent group therapy are as follows:

1. 1. Be open and honest about your feelings as you are experiencing them. The chemically dependent person is usually out of touch with his feelings, and does not know how to identify them. The purpose here is to help the patient integrate his feelings and his behavior, and express himself in an appropriate manner.

2. Do not hide behind anger and aggressive behavior. The purpose is to require that the patient learn to express a broader range of feelings and behaviors.

3. Learn to confront others appropriately when they offend you, or behave in a way which is self-defeating. This value teaches the patient to take some responsibility for the welfare of his fellow patients. The patients learn not to ignore something they believe is not right.

4. Accept confrontation from others when they tell you about something you have done which they did not like, or was inappropriate. This can be a very difficult value for a dependent adolescent to accept. Group therapy can plant the seeds for learning this behavior, but practicing it outside of group will take some time to master.

5. Accept your powerlessness over drugs and the unmanageability of your life. This can ba a particularly difficult value for the adolescent to accept. The last thing any adolescent wants to admit is that he is powerless. Yet, this is the one feeling they tend to experience most often, and most want to deny. It may be that the older, more mature group members will be the only ones who can truly understand this concept. Early adolescents may tend to maintain a strong resistance to this notion of powerlessness. The wise counselor will realize that it is the intellectual limitations of the early adolescent which interfere with their understanding and acceptance.

Conforming to these values will take the dependent youngster a long way towards recovery. But, the counselor must also realize that each adolescent will need to retain some amount of individual integrity. It is not healthy to give up all of one's defenses. Just because a patient puts up some resistance to accepting the values of the group does not necessarily imply he is not getting well. The counselor must carefully assess a given adolescent's limitations and adjust therapy accordingly. Some adolescents may be returning to a home, or social environment where they must retain some of their defenses just to survive.

This issue of the personal defense system raises the issue of when group therapy can be dangerous to the welfare of an adolescent. Some adolescents simply may not have the ego strength to cope with the intensity of the group. Younger adolescents are especially vulnerable in groups, and the makeup of the group must be considered carefully before placing this age group in it. On the other hand, adolescents can become so embracing of the group's influence that they cannot make any decisions on their own. Some individuals will desire group acceptance so intensely that they will conform to anything. This person is very vulnerable after treatment, in that he may simply go along with whatever group he should happen to fall in with.

Finally, it is the author's belief that group therapists must treat their patients with the utmost respect and concern for their welfare. Because groups can be so intensely powerful, they can also do great damage to the individual. No counselor should ever condone the occurrence of verbal or physical abuse during group therapy. Some individuals may need intense confrontation to break through their defense system. But, the counselor must carefully evaluate whether the individual can survive the confrontation. Just because a drug-addicted 17-year-old presents a tougher exterior, it does not necessarily mean she can cope with an unrelenting attack upon her defense system.

The author recommends that all counselors contemplate the potential consequences of their actions, and those of the members of the group. The author always uses the image of himself on the witness stand being cross-examined by the prosecuting attorney. "Dr. Ellis, did you realize the patient was at risk for suicide when you allowed the group to attack her so mercilessly?" Would you be prepared to answer such a question? It is obviously better never to find yourself in a position to have to answer such a question.

Levels of Group Therapy

Drug dependent and abusing adolescents can benefit from a variety of group experiences. Group does not have to be limited to the intense, confrontive type described above. Less intensive environments can be quite helpful, depending upon the needs of the individual. This section will briefly discuss four different group environments, and the structure and purposes of such groups.

Educational Groups:

The general purpose of this type of group is to share information about a variety of issues, such as effects of drugs, sexuality, communication skills, health, understanding adults, or school performance. These groups can be offered in either an inpatient or outpatient environment. Usually these groups are more informal, encouraging discussion and may even involve group activities (field trips, structured tasks, or games).

Outpatient Group Therapy:

The purposes of this type of group would not be particularly different from those of inpatient groups. The five values mentioned above would also pertain to this group. However, the intensity of this group experience would always be less. When a counselor is unable to observe the behavioral consequences of group interaction, he must be more careful to contain and limit confrontations. In an outpatient setting, adolescents should not be allowed to leave the office in an unstable condition. The counselor may have to spend additional time with a patient after group, if the experience was particularly traumatic. In this situation, the counselor simply has less control over the outside environment. Progress may be slower in this setting, as well. Finally, adolescents who come to outpatient groups are usually better adjusted and have fewer dysfunctional behaviors than those found in hospital environments.

Inpatient Groups:

Many of the purposes of this type of group have already been discussed. Again, this setting will focus upon confronting, containing and changing those seriously dysfunctional behaviors. These are the behaviors which make it impossible for the individual to remain drug free, and function adequately outside of the treatment environment. The structure usually involves daily group meetings of varying lengths. The group is often used as a problem-solving arena when there has been a conflict on the unit. The rules for behavior in group are usually quite specific and strictly enforced.

Alcoholics Anonymous:

AA is both helpful as an educational environment, and as a "therapeutic" environment. As was the case with Billy, AA was useful to him, in that he learned about where he was heading and about alcoholism. In Richard's case, AA would become essential for him to maintain sobriety beyond treatment. But, AA is not for everyone. Many adolescents have great difficulty adapting to the program of AA and the people they meet there. In many communities there are no young people's AA meetings. These adolescents are forced to attend meetings with adults, and they generally do not mix well. If AA is to be helpful to an adolescent, it must be adaptive to his needs and developmental level. But, most importantly, AA provides the dependent adolescent with a new, positive social environment which supports staying sober and learning to have fun without drugs. Many communities with young people's AA will organize activites (i.e., dances, trips, etc.) for their members. Here they can socialize without fear of having to deal with the temptations of alcohol and drugs.

When Groups Fail

As mentioned above, group therapy is not always indicated when designing a treatment program for a chemically dependent adolescent. To prevent groups from failing, it is best to give serious consideration to the purposes for a group and who should attend. The following is a list of factors to consider when determining whether to place a given adolescent in group.

1. What is the child's developmental level intellectually and emotionally? Children under the age of 13 do not typically do well in inpatient group therapy. Also, this age group does not do well in groups with broad age ranges. They do not possess the insight and ego strength to "compete" with older adolescents. Educational groups are usually more effective with the younger adolescents.
2. When placing a child in an outpatient group, the counselor must consider the quality of his family environment. Will group therapy raise issues which will only make things worse at home? Can the home environment support the goals of the group therapy? For instance, will the parents tolerate their child becoming more expressive of his feelings? It may be necessary to work with the parents first, before placing their child in a group.
3. Is the adolescent truly dependent upon drugs, or is he an abuser? It is best to place an abusing adolescent in a homeogeneous group. The goals of group therapy with dependent adolescents will differ from those of abusing adolescents.

Group therapy is generally indicated for most dependent adolescents, but because of its potential power, must be employed cautiously. The group counselor must be sensitive to issues of adolescent development. He must be able to identify the nature of an adolescent's internal struggles, and those with the outside world. With this knowledge, the counselor must then determine if the group environment is the best place to resolve these struggles. Often, a counselor may unknowingly force an adolescent into exposing himself in group when he is actually unable to cope with this. An adolescent patient may come to trust his counselor intensely, and do whatever he asks. Because of this eagerness to please the counselor, the patient may take a risk larger than he can afford. The adolescent may need considerable preparation before he can share a particularly sensitive issue in group (i.e. incest, sexual abuse, or criminal activity).

Chapter 6

Family Therapy

Little happens to us, or because of us, without first coming from the roots of our family heritage. With families being such strong influences, it would be incomprehensible to leave them out of our therapeutic strategies. However, just including families in the treatment of chemically dependent adolescents is not enough. As a therapist, stepping into the life of a patient's family can be a delicate and arduous experience. Knowing where to step, and where not to step, is required of the therapist who wishes to work with families.

This chapter does not attempt to address all there is to know about family therapy. There are numerous other sources which are more complete on this subject, and will be referenced. This chapter will offer an overview of family dynamics, how to treat the families of chemically dependent adolescents, and procedures for re-unifying the family system.

Patterns of Interaction

What is a family? A family is generally a group of people who live together and are interdependent upon each other for survival. However, living together is not necessarily a prerequisite to be a family. There can be extended members of the family who live elsewhere, or are even deceased. But all can still have influence upon the individual members.

Family members occupy various family positions which are in a state of interdependency. A change in the position, status, behavior, or role of one member leads to change in the behavior of other members. The family is a boundary-maintaining unit, with varying degress of rigidity and permeability in defining the family and non-family world. The family is also an adaptive and equilibrium-seeking unit with patterns of interaction repeating themselves over time. Finally, the family is a task-performing unit that meets both requirements of external agencies representing society, and also the internal needs and demands of its members.

Within any family system, there are various and specific roles which get assigned, inherited, or acquired by individual members. These roles are interdependent upon each other, and as time goes by these roles can become intractible. The work of Sharon Wegscheider (1981) has identified five common roles in alcoholic families: Enabler; Hero; Scapegoat; Lost Child; and Mascot. Wegscheider proposes that these roles help to support the family's alcoholic. Usually this alcoholic is an adult. The chemically dependent adolescent can often develop out of one of these five roles. There is some crossover between these roles and the identities mentioned in Chapter One: Achievement Identity; Foreclosure; Diffusion Identity; and Moratoriums. There seems to be apparent similarity between the Scapegoats and the Moratoriums, and the Lost Children and the Diffusion Identities.

Whether it is the adult who is chemically dependent or the adolescent, this role tends to carry with it considerable power within the family system. Most families are reluctant to jettison a member just because he has problems, or misbehaves. So, the family tries to adapt to its wayward member and, if possible, contain the problem. But, by doing so, the family also develops what is called "co-dependent" behaviors (Elkin, 1984). This co-dependent behavior may be characterized by denying obvious intoxication, blaming someone else, or minimizing the seriousness of troublesome behavior.

The therapist who engages the adolescent's family in therapy will more than likely focus upon altering the family's patterns of interaction. When an adolescent is acting out inappropriately, the insightful therapist will look at the parental relationship as a possible source of the conflict. An adolescent's immature, disruptive behavior may be a representation of an immature relationship between her parents (Roberts, 1982). If a child is to cope competently with life's struggles she is somewhat dependent upon her parents as a reliable source of support. If mom and dad are continually locked in battle when their child needs attention, then maladjustment may follow. There seems to be a strong correlation between adolescent drug abuse and broken homes, irresponsible parents, or alcoholic parents (Jurich, 1985).

All of us have had unpleasant experiences due to our parents. Most adults or adolescents have, at some time, observed their parents argue. Yet, most of us survive this and come to realize that life is not perfect. We insulate ourselves from the minor conflicts. We learn to let a certain amount of this roll off our backs. To become chemically dependent does not require a specific amount of parental conflict or family discord. Each person has a threshold for tolerating interactional dysfunction within his/her family. This threshold will vary from person to person. Some of us can bear more than others, or have better coping mechanisms than our friends and relatives.

When the therapist enters into the family system, it is a good idea to retrace the family's steps to see how they have interacted recently and in the more distant past. Shapiro emphasizes that once conflicts have been uncovered, the therapist should work towards reducing resistance and maximize positive, agreed upon changes (Shapiro, 1977). The majority of the changes generally need to occur within the marital relationship. In some instances, rearranging the way a family interacts will enable it to handle and contain an adolescent's drug abuse.

Simply altering the patterns of interaction will not always be sufficient, as was the case in Sharon's and Richard's families. However, changing the way a family interacts is still indicated, in order to ensure the overall success of the adolescent's treatment (Stanton, 1982).

Unfortunately, not all "family therapists" realize the shortcomings of their strategic and systems approaches to therapy. It is critical to the welfare of the chemically dependent adolescent that the therapist know when to attack the dependency directly (Ellis, 1986). Just laboring over the way the parents fight will not necessarily interrupt the ongoing drug use of an adolescent addict. But, as was true in Billy's case, changing the way the parents interacted, and giving them information, helped them to contain the problem on their own.

When and How to Involve the Family

In nearly all cases, the families of drug-abusing and addicted adolescents should be involved in therapy. Everyone in the family has been affected. Each member has been hurt, ashamed, angry and scared, due to the adolescent's drug use. Because of this, every member of the family needs some kind of attention, if only to make everyone aware that chemical dependency is a family problem. It is not uncommon for counselors to discover that family members do not believe they have anything to do with their drug-using member. "He is the one with the problem, not me. Why do I have to come see a counselor?" This is a frequent statement made by the siblings of a chemically dependent adolescent. Chemically dependent families are often disconnected, each individual having little to do with the others (Coleman, 1976).

As mentioned earlier, drug abusing adolescents often have parents who are less than effective at doing their job. The sensitive therapist will wish to support the parents, and elevate them back to a position of authority. It is not recommended for the counselor to take over the parent's job, but to help them improve their parenting. Dropping off the unhappy teenager at the clinic, or hospital is not going to adequately solve the problem (Ellis, 1984). Parents and children need information about drug abuse and dependency and how it affects their lives. Misunderstanding the nature of their child's problem, for the parent, can be nearly as damaging as the actual use of drugs. Many authors have attempted to write books and pamphlets informing parents about drug and alcohol use. Stanton Peele's little book, *Don't Panic: A Parent's Guide to Understanding and Preventing Alcohol and Drug Abuse* (Peele, 1983), is a helpful publication. Other programs have focused on helping parents learn how to talk with their children about drug use. *Talking With Your Kids About Alcohol* (Prevention Research Institute), is an excellent example of just such a program.

Finally, families need to be involved in the treatment of their adolescent, simply to support him through a very difficult stage of his life. Research has demonstrated repeatedly that chemically dependent patients stay sober longer if their families actively support them during and after treatment (Stanton, 1982).

When Families Should Not Be Involved

There are some circumstances when an adolescent's family should not participate with him/her in therapy. If family members are in critical need of therapy, they may not be in a position to help their dependent member. Some home environments can be so pathologically dysfunctional that they would only tend to make things worse, if involved in therapy.

A family with an alcoholic parent can often find it difficult to respond appropriately to the needs of a drug dependent child. The parent's alcoholism disrupts the hierarchy in the parental authority, and, in effect, can neutralize Mom and Dad. This is only compounded if the alcoholic parent is also a single parent, with custody of the dependent adolescent.

Families under exceptional stress can also find themselves unable to help the adolescent needing treatment. This stressful event, or circumstance, can supercede all other problems. The death of a parent, or the divorce of the parents, can render even the strongest families nearly helpless. The family may even send a message to the addicted adolescent, "Your problems are less important than the immediate crisis, so either straighten up, or handle it on your own." Usually under these conditions, the adolescent will either run away from treatment, or the family will pull him out themselves.

In some cases, the author has seen drug abusing and dependent adolescents temporarily improve due to the family's crisis. In these cases, it is the family's crisis which overrides that of the adolescent. In some instances, this improvement lasted only a few months, and in others the adolescent discontinued drug use altogether. But, more often, the adolescent would continue his drug use. The dependency problem would go underground for a while until the family recovered from its setback. This can be a very discouraging development for a counselor, and keeping the teenager in treatment can be quite difficult. Treatment personnel are inclined to release the patients out of sympathy and on the promise he will return after everything is settled. If at all possible, it is best to try to keep the adolescent in treatment. The counselor may have to offer the family other options or resources in order to help them deal with their respective problem.

Finally, and unfortunately, some parents simply do not care about their child. The uninvolved and irresponsible parent can prove to be a burden to family therapy. This is a difficult judgment for a counselor to make. Some would like to believe that with encouragement and education the uncaring parent would experience a metamorphosis. Occasionally this happens, but more often the parent is glad to let his child be someone else's problem. It is a sad reality, yet a child from this type of home may be better off living somewhere else where he is cared for.

Therapeutic Contracts

In the early stages of family therapy, the counselor is advised to negotiate a therapeutic contract with the family. This contract dictates the course of therapy/treatment and what is expected of everyone, including the counselor (Meeks, 1973). The contract may be written, or verbal, but everyone should agree to the conditions.

A counselor may contract with the family for such things as the length of therapy. If it is outpatient, then the family needs to know approximately how long they will be coming. Of course, it can be difficult to pinpoint a specific ending for therapy. However, the counselor can suggest, "We will meet for six sessions and stop to evaluate what we have accomplished." This leaves open the option to renegotiate goals, continue meeting, or terminate.

In a hospital environment, the family needs to know the specific length of treatment, the length of the aftercare program, the amount of family counseling involved, and any other additional services which may be involved. These facts must be checked against the family's ability to pay for the services. It is best to have no hidden agendas or costs when negotiating a contract with a family.

Finally, the counselor should negotiate a family contract regarding some basic ground rules. These rules may involve how the family will communicate with each other. The rules may have to do with home maintainance, who is to do what within the family's home (i.e., housekeeping, curfew, decision-making, etc.). How the counselor's fee will be paid may even be negotiated with the family. The author knows of one counselor who negotiated a contract where every member of the family was responsible for paying a portion of the counseling fee.

The Systems and Strategic Models

The systems and strategic models of family therapy are two compatible approaches which focus upon the ways families interact and how they are structured. The systems therapist will address helping families change the way they interact, the belief being that a change in the patterns of interaction will result in the family learning to function more effectively. Increased efficiency does not necessarily require that the family possess new insights. The therapist may simply want them to behave differently in specific situations. Insight may come later, almost unconsciously, as the family adapts to a new way of interacting.

The strategic therapist is less concerned with patterns of interaction, but more with the fundamental structure of the family system. Structure may have to do with the nature of the family's hierarchy of authority. Or, structure may address conflict within the marital relationship, which results in both parents becoming ineffective as executives of the family. Sometimes a chemically dependent child can come to wield too much power in the family. With one or more weak parents, the dependent child may be able to override parental authority. This is usually compounded by two parents who are rarely in agreement about anything. The strategic therapist would intervene upon such a system by possibly assigning the parents new roles. Or, the therapist might try a more provocative approach, and challenge the child to become a more dominant figure in his family. This paradoxical maneuver will be discussed later in this chapter. Regardless of the technique, the strategic therapist wishes to change the structure of the family.

Systems and strategic therapists have essentially the same goals —to cause change in families. The methods are only slightly different, and often cross over in how they appear to the outward observer. The purpose of this section is to present some basic concepts and methods which could be employed by both therapies. It is common for most family therapists to employ both models interchangeably.

What are the purposes of family therapy? The following list presents some broad purposes for therapy with chemically dependent families.

1. To aid family members to understand their alignments, agreements and roles.
2. To intervene into destructive agreements among family members and to facilitate constructive agreements.
3. To shift communication patterns between family members.
4. To facilitate the family's understanding of the relationship between family interaction and the presenting problem.
5. To enable the family to change its interaction with the chemically dependent client in a manner which facilitates and maximizes the potential for change in the client.
6. To establish, with active family consent, appropriate goals for individual and family growth.
7. To develop the respective family member's capacity to perceive his or her influence on other family member's behaviors.
8. To develop each family member's understanding of how his or her own behavior is influenced by other members of the family.

When a therapist begins therapy with a family, she, in effect, becomes a defacto member of that family. Besides assessing how each family member influences another, the therapist must also assess how she influences and is influenced by the family. While observing the flow of interaction in the family, the therapist is assessing the "communication loops." The family has an historical sense which the therapist does not. Certain loops of information may be more meaningful than others. As a newcomer, the therapist is advised to spend a considerable amount of time observing and listening in the early sessions.

Family Rules

While observing a family's communication loops, the therapist must also listen for family rules. Every family has a set of rules by which they live. Some of these rules are obvious, or overt, such as, "You will not use certain swear words in this family."

Other rules are less obvious; these are covert rules. A covert rule might be that no one is ever to mention Dad's drinking. These rules influence the internal operation of the family and must be understood by the therapist.

Families are also governed by extra family rules. Extra family rules are those that exist beyond the boundaries of the family, but have somehow been incorporated and influence behavior. An extra family rule may be something that the greater community has implicitly agreed upon. An example may be that Friday night is the mens' night out.

These rules help to maintain a level of homeostasis within the family system. All families strive for a homeostatic balance. Homeostasis will bring to rest those reciprocal functions which can drain energy from a family. A reciprocal function might be that little Sally will continue to fail in school as long as Dad gets drunk. Sally's failures in school help to take attention away from Dad's drinking and focuses it upon her. Somehow, Dad has to pay Sally back. Dad may be more permissive with Sally than her mother when she wants something.

Alliances and Triangulation

Within each family, there are dyadic relationships which may be more significant to the individuals involved than other relationships. Mother and son may experience an alliance with each other, a bond which may be even closer than the marital bond. Alliance is a process which family members live out mutually felt, and, as such, understood roles (e.g. mother and son do not criticize each other in front of Father). Alliances are a normal phenomenon within the family system. However, these alliances can contribute to, or become a result of, a dysfunction somewhere else. If the marital relationship is basically nonfunctional, the parents may align themselves closely with one, or more of the children, to compensate for this. This can place unnecessary stress on the children. A given child may develop too much power in the family, and the other parent may feel blocked out. This is commonly referred to as triangulation.

Triangulation is the process by which influence is exercised beyond the level of the dyad. For example, a drug-abusing adolescent may align himself with a parent as a mechanism for avoiding confrontation with both parents. If a drug-abusing son were to align himself with Mom, and remain hostile to Dad, then when he got into trouble he could use this alliance to triangulate out (neutralize) Dad. This is a common occurence in families with chemically dependent adolescents. One parent believes the child is being persecuted by his, or her, spouse. As a result, the aligned parent will defend the child against the nonaligned parent. In this situation, neither parent may see how his/her child is manipulating them, and how this protects the child's drug use.

Intergenerational Influences

Most practitioners and researchers in the field of chemical dependency agree that familial and genetic influences are factors in the development of the disease. Because of this, it is recommended that counselors do a thorough family history as a part of any family treatment program. Familial values around alcohol and drug use are strong influences in the lives of adolescents. It is important, as a counselor, to learn how these values are learned and passed on to other generations. In some families, it is nearly impossible to escape chemical dependency. The family described next was just such a family.

The Anderson family was a family who came to counseling due to the problems of their youngest daughter. This daughter was three months pregnant, and had just recently dropped out of school. The daughter's attitude was disturbing to her parents and they wanted to try to do something to help her. The counselor decided to do a genogram with the family to learn about their past. A genogram is similar to a family tree. The counselor wished to diagram the structure of the family, including present relationships, as well as those of earlier generations. The completed genogram is shown in Fig. 1.

From doing this genogram, the counselor discovered some rather amazing information. Mr. Anderson was raised by two alcoholic parents, who are presently 76 years of age, and have been sober for the past 20 years. Mr. Anderson had one brother who died at the age of 54 due to alcoholism. Mrs. Anderson grew up in the Morrison family, and both of her parents are practicing alcoholics. Her mother is 68 and her father is 70.

Mrs. Anderson's mother had an incestual relationship with her alcoholic brother shortly after marrying her husband. This child was rejected by the family and placed in a children's home. This child became alcoholic, and has been sober now for 15 years. Mrs. Anderson also had another brother who is an addicted gambler, and a sister who is a practicing alcoholic. Finally, Mrs. Anderson had one other brother who died at the age of 6 years.

Mr. and Mrs. Anderson met at a dance while she was still in high school. Mrs. Anderson was desperate to get out of her parent's house and felt that marriage was the only way. She tried hard to get pregnant by Mr. Anderson, but failing at this, she dropped out of high school and asked him to marry her. At first, Mr. Anderson balked at the idea; he was having too much fun drinking and running around. Then Mrs. Anderson lied to him and told him she thought she was pregnant. At this point, Mr. Anderson quickly agreed to get married. After marriage, Mrs. Anderson confessed she had tricked him, and from there the relationship deteriorated. Mr. Anderson continued to drink and run around, while Mrs. Anderson stayed home and drank alone.

Mr. Anderson's drinking eventually got him into trouble at work, and he was told to quit drinking or resign. Mr. Anderson started

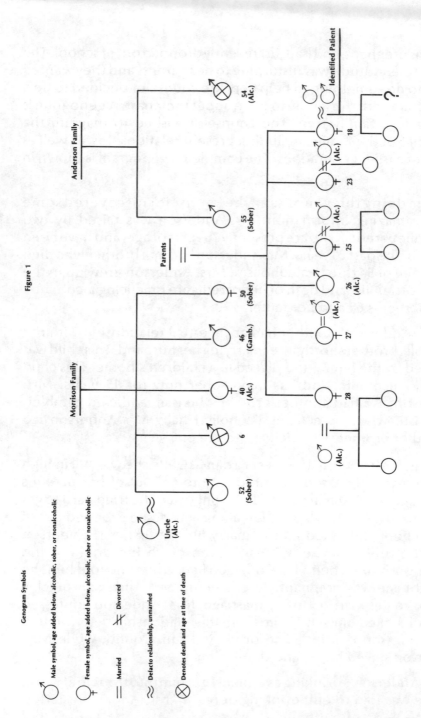

Figure 1

Genogram Symbols

○↗ Male symbol, age added below, alcoholic, sober, or nonalcoholic

○⊢ Female symbol, age added below, alcoholic, sober or nonalcoholic

= Married   ≠ Divorced

≈ Defacto relationship, unmarried

⊗ Denotes death and age at time of death

going to AA and Mrs. Anderson went along with him, out of curiosity. Mr. Anderson quit drinking and shortly thereafter Mrs. Anderson did the same.

Mr. and Mrs. Anderson eventually had six children, five girls and one boy. The Anderson's oldest daughter (28) got pregnant at 16, dropped out of high school, married an alcoholic, and had two children. The next-oldest daughter (27) got pregnant at 17, dropped out of high school and married an alcoholic. The Anderson's only son (26) dropped out of high school at 16, is an alcoholic and bounces from one job to another. The Anderson's 25-year-old daughter got pregnant at 15, dropped out of high school, married an alcoholic, had a second child and then divorced her husband. The 23-year-old daughter got pregnant, dropped out of high school, married an alcoholic and then divorced him. This daughter was living with her parents when they came in for counseling. The youngest daughter (identified patient) was 15 at the time they entered counseling and had already dropped out of high school. During the course of therapy, this daughter gave birth to a son, but did not get married to the child's father. Shortly after giving birth, this daughter became sexually involved with another boy, and at 18 was suspecting that she was again pregnant.

Not all genograms are as discouraging as the Andersons, but their's is a good example of the compelling influences a family can have upon its members. The intergenerational influences of this family system were awsome, and the individual members were powerless to resist. The parents had decided to take a stand with their youngest daughter to try to keep her from repeating the same mistakes everyone else had. As can be seen from the genogram, the parent's efforts were only partially successful.

The First Session

Because families can present such complex problems and convoluted interdependencies, beginning therapy with them can be overwhelming. This is why, at first, the counselor simply wants to collect information. The counselor should assess the drug abuse patterns of all family members, including the extended family. Also, the counselor wants to observe the family's patterns of interaction during the session, as well as have them describe what goes on at home. The counselor certainly wants to assess his relationship to the family, how he feels about them, and how they seem to feel about him.

Joining the family system can be difficult for even the most experienced counselor. This is a deeply personal experience. To enter into a family as a counselor is to come to know some of their most intimate secrets. Regardless of how dysfunctional the family is, the counselor must always respect the relative integrity of the family. Imagine yourself in their situation, and how difficult it might be to do anything different from what they are presently doing.

Family Therapy Techniques

The specific techniques discussed here can be employed in a variety of therapeutic situations, not limited to family therapy. But, the techniques mentioned are essential at some point or another during family therapy. Any counselor attempting family therapy must have a working knowledge of the following techniques.

Re-framing

This technique's purpose is to help families to come to a new understanding, or perspective on an old problem. The counselor attempts to re-frame, or change the family's way of viewing a problem. The re-frame places the problem in either a more positive light, or within a more manageable context. The family may view a child's specific behavior as simply defiant and blatantly rebellious. The counselor may re-frame the behavior as a response to some internal family conflict. Rather than focusing energy upon changing the child alone, the family will come to understand that they may all have to make some changes.

Go-between

Sometimes in family therapy, the counselor will have to act as a conduit of communication for those members who cannot, or will not, talk directly to each other. Individual's communication skills may prevent family members from effectively articulating what they feel. As an example, a counselor may encourage a father and son to continue talking beyond the point where they would usually walk away from each other. The counselor interprets, de-fuses and facilitates ongoing communication when the individuals would prefer to give up.

Empowering

The technique of empowering has to do with aiding those family members who are quiet and withdrawn to more fully participate in therapy. Some family members will clearly be more dominant than others, at home and in therapy. The counselor must be aware of all the members of the family during the course of therapy. Everyone should be heard from, and it may fall upon the counselor to empower the more subdued members of the family. With adolescents and children, just asking them to share their thoughts and feelings may not be adequate. At times, the counselor may need to speak for the children, acting as an advocate for what he believes they are thinking. For instance, the counselor may say, "From the look on Sally's face (13-year-old), I would say she feels hurt by that last comment. Is that right Sally?"

Paradox

The use of paradox in family therapy with the chemically dependent is a provocative technique which should be used with a reasonable amount of caution. Paradox can be defined as two truths in seeming opposition to each other, or a statement which is apparently contradictory. Much of human behavior is full of paradox. We frequently behave in ways contradictory to what we say, and believe. The counselor using paradox is attempting to prescribe the exaggeration of an already absurd or dysfunctional behavior. For example, a counselor may assign two intensely "co-dependent" parents to try harder to control their drug-abusing child.

The use of paradox should be used only when other methods have failed. A counselor would only prescribe parents to control their child more if he felt it was the only way to demonstrate to them their powerlessness. Paradox can easily backfire if the counselor has not thoroughly assessed the family's readiness for such an assignment. To some parents, hearing that they should try harder to control their child may simply prolong therapy. If the parents have not truly tried everything they could, trying harder may make some sense to them. However, to assign parents to intensify an already absurd behavior must be done when the counselor is certain they are at the end of their rope.

Family Sculpture

Family sculpture is a therapeutic technique which has been perfected by Virginia Satir. The technique, or method, helps families to dramatically act out and represent specific interactional dynamics. A counselor will usually assign one member of the family to physically position the other members in a way that represents how they see the inter-relationships within the family. The counselor may ask a family member to position their family to represent a specific conflict which is being discussed in therapy.

As an example, a younger child may position her family to represent how her drug-abusing brother dominates the rest of the family. This allows the family to experience and understand their problem in another way. Some family members may have good verbal skills and can articulate well what they feel. Other members have different skills, especially the younger children, and family sculpture offers them an opportunity to express themselves. Family sculpture can bring new insight to a confused situation and sometimes even offer a possible solution.

Resistant Families

It is common in chemically dependent family systems for the counselor to experience resistance in getting all of them to come in for therapy. When adolescents are involved, it is usually the mother who brings the child in for therapy. The father may resist coming in because he does not believe in counseling, has given up on his child, or is chemically dependent himself. In other situations, both parents may bring their child in but resist bringing in the rest of the family. They may say, "The other children are just fine and we didn't want to expose them to this." Regardless of the circumstances, it is important that the counselor insist that all members of the family come in. To do a complete assessment, the counselor must see everyone in order to understand the inter-relatedness of each member of the family to the presenting problem.

The earlier in therapy the counselor demands to see the rest of the family, the more likely they will come in. The counselor must realize this may create a crisis within the family. Usually, with chemically dependency it is a crisis of denial. Those absent members may be the ones who most strongly deny the adolescent's dependency. Therapy can be futile if these people are not present. Also, it is imperative that the counselor's agency support the necessity for involving all members of the family therapy. This leads to more success in getting families to come in.

Sometimes it may be necessary for the counselor to contact the missing family members directly. This way the counselor can be sure that the members present in therapy do not sabotage efforts to bring others in. A counselor may call an absent father and say, "In order to help your son, I need you to be here for the sessions. I'm sure you want to do anything you can to see that your son gets his problems resolved." Another maneuver may be to say, "Your wife and son have been talking about you here. It seems to me that you ought to be here to present your side of things, especially since we are going to be making some changes, and I'm sure you will want some imput into this."

Terminating Therapy

Ideally, family therapy is terminated when the family and the counselor agree that their goals have been completed satisfactorily. However, with chemically dependent adolescents, family therapy may prove to be inadequate and a referral to a more intense treatment program may be necessary. Listed below are some issues to consider when preparing to terminate family counseling.

1. Has the family reached its agreed upon goals?
2. Are individual family members emotionally prepared to accept termination?
3. Does the family seem to understand the process, what has happened to them, and do they possess a sense of completeness?

4. Discuss conditions under which the family might re-enter therapy.
5. Summarize what has happened, and explain they will still have problems in the future, but they are able now to handle them on their own.
6. Partial goal completion can be acceptable if the family has redefined future expectations.
7. If necessary, fully explain the need to refer them to a residential treatment program, or some other therapist.
8. Request that the family re-contact you (by phone, letter, or personal visit) in approximately six months to let you know how they are doing.

Chapter 7

Treatment Outcomes and Follow-Up

What happens to the chemically dependent adolescent after completing treatment may be the most critical period for this population. Those treatment programs which bother to do follow-up studies have been discovering some very disturbing information. It appears that nearly 50% of those adolescents who complete treatment return to using drugs again within six months, or less. These statistics may indicate that something is lacking in the treatment program. But, it also seems quite apparent that the post-treatment period needs additional attention.

This chapter will address procedures for determining appropriate outcome goals for adolescents. It is the author's belief that counselors may set unrealistic goals for adolescents, which can result in an unsuccessful recovery. Also, this chapter will discuss doing follow-up counseling, using Richard's case as an example.

What are appropriate outcome goals for different adolescent ages?

When determining outcome goals for chemically dependent adolescents, the counselor must consider the true age at which the patient is functioning. Chemically dependent adolescents are typically not functioning at their chronological age level. This population is generally running behind their actual age. The following is a breakdown of some typical outcomes one can expect from adolescents of differing ages. The reader should keep in mind that a given 15-year-old may actually be more like a 12-year-old emotionally.

Early Adolescence (11-14 years)

1. This group can be expected to develop a basic understanding of the harmful effects of drugs.
2. These children can be expected to learn to identify and discuss their feelings.
3. This age group can be expected to understand the value of abstinence and make a commitment to this.
4. This group can begin to form a more positive peer group.
5. This group can be expected to understand and obey parental rules.
6. This group should not get involved in intense romantic relationships.

Middle Adolescence (15-17 years)

7. This group should minimally adhere to the expectations 1 through 6.
8. These adolescents should be able to accept full responsibility for their behavior and the consequences.
9. This group can develop a basic understanding of the principles of Alcoholics Anonymous.
10. This population can begin to set personal goals (i.e., school, relationships and employment).

Late Adolescence (18-21 years)

11. Minimally, 1 through 10.
12. This age group can begin to integrate knowledge and experience into a personal belief system.
13. Understand and practice the AA program.
14. This group should be capable of experimenting with the formation of longer term romantic relationships.
15. Finally, this group can begin the process of making plans for leaving home.

These goals may seem modest, in light of the numerous and complex problems the chemically dependent adolescent can manifest. However, this population is in need of long-term therapy which should extend well beyond the relatively brief hospitalization. Patients in out-patient therapy may require less intense programs, but long-term care may still be indicated.

In Richard's case, he was clearly operating at a developmental level below his chronological age. Although he was chronologically within the middle adolescent range, Richard was actually functioning more like an early adolescent. When Richard came to me for follow-up counseling, it was clear that the half-way house staff were expecting more from him than he was capable of delivering. Richard had learned that he had feelings, and that he was not very good at identifying them, nor communicating them. When Richard would talk of his feelings, it was in a rather stilted and aloof manner.

Richard had little trouble accepting that he could no longer use alcohol and drugs. Also, Richard accepted that he needed to go to AA meetings every day, once he was released from the halfway house. This was necessary, primarily to structure Richard's time when he was not in school. Richard did not fully grasp the concepts of AA, but he was willing to obey the rules outlined by his AA sponsor. This person was valuable to Richard in that he could call on him whenever he was needed.

Because of Richard's addiction to sex, he was also to abstain from any sexual contact with girls. Actually, it was best for Richard to avoid any romantic relationships with girls for at least the first six months after leaving the halfway house. Richard became involved with a support group for adolescents who had committed sexual assault. This group was critical to Richard's recovery because it allowed him to better understand his self-centered attitudes about sex. The group also helped Richard begin to understand how little he respected women in general. Richard needed to learn a new set of socially appropriate behaviors for use with girls.

Returning to school was difficult for Richard because he had never experienced success there. Previously, school was just a game to Richard. Now Richard was afraid of school and intimidated by the teachers. Without drugs, Richard had few methods for dealing with teachers in an appropriate manner. Richard had to be taught how to talk to teachers, how to understand what they want and how to study. Richard could not just openly state his feelings like he had been encouraged to do while in the treatment center. Richard had to learn how to be tactful.

Richard wanted only to graduate from high school, he did not care to go on to college afterwards. This seemed realistic to me. However, Richard was still a dreamer and wanted to become a stuntman in Hollywood after high school. This goal had to be altered somewhat. Richard needed to look at alternative goals which might parallel the life of a stuntman. The Marine Corps was something that seemed appealing to Richard.

Finally, Richard had a distorted concept of money. He had always had money, but had never earned any. Later in recovery, Richard began looking for a job after some careful coaching on how to interview and fill out an application. Richard did find a job in a fast food restaurant which he kept for a while. Richard did not keep the job long, but it was a positive beginning.

When is it necessary to diagnose an adolescent chemically dependent?

Labeling an adolescent "chemically dependent" should be given careful consideration. The adolescent should match up with the criteria in Chapter Three before assigning this label. In Richard's case, there was no doubt, and it was important to his recovery that he understand his condition. But, with Billy the label was not appropriate; he did not fit the criteria. Also, Billy would only be taking on another unnecessary problem if he had to accept that he was chemically dependent.

Sometimes a clinician is unsure if a particular adolescent patient is chemically dependent or not. In such cases, it is best to get another opinion. If the adolescent is 13 years of age, then it may be premature to assign this label. And finally, it is generally best to try the least restrictive treatment environment first. It is better to undertreat an adolescent and then adjust upwards, than it is to overtreat and then try to undo the possible damage this could cause.

Occasionally, counselors may feel the diagnosis of chemical

dependency is inappropriate for a given adolescent client. However, the counselor may experience pressure from others to find the client dependent. It may be parents, school systems, courts, or even insurance companies that require such a diagnosis. Because the diagnosis of chemical dependency can be such a burdensome label with which to live, the counselor must be quite sure before assigning it. If the external pressure is too great, then the counselor may want to refer the adolescent somewhere else for another opinion. On the contrary, some counselors may be quite certain of their client's dependency, but find that no one else will believe it could be true. This may be due to the denial that an adolescent could be dependent upon drugs. Often a struggle will follow the diagnosis, and the counselor will have to be persistent in asserting his recommendation.

How involved should a child's family become in an adolescent's recovery?

In the case of a late adolescent, the family may not need to be intensely involved in his recovery. However, it is recommended that the family go to Al-Anon and that the parents also attend parent support groups if they are available. A 19-year-old should begin to take responsibility for managing his own life, as well as his recovery.

The younger the adolescent, the more involved the family should become in the recovery process. Family therapy is strongly recommended for any families where the adolescent is still living at home. The counselor cannot follow his client around 24 hours a day. Obviously, the parents cannot do this either. But, the parents will need to monitor their child's progress and help him to rebuild his life again.

Sometimes families can become too involved in the recovery of their adolescent members. Parents who were too protective before treatment are not going to give this up easily. Ongoing family therapy will need to focus upon allowing the child some room within which to grow and make mistakes. Sometimes parents will watch their dependent child like hawks and swoop down on them for the most minor infraction. This tends to set up a repetition of the previous pattern, which was not helping the child to become more independent.

Then, on the other hand, some parents will simply not accept their child's dependency. This was the case with Richard's mother. She would not go to Al-Anon meetings because she did not feel she needed them, and she did not really believe in what she heard at the meetings. Richard's mother had for so long overlooked and denied Richard's problems, that she could not easily turn over a new leaf. Family therapy was instrumental in helping her to understand that her son had to attend AA meetings and sexual addiction meetings to stay "straight."

Also Richard's mother was having trouble getting over her husband's death. She was angry, but not quite sure at whom she was angry. She tended to express most of her anger at Richard, but she later discovered much of the anger was for her husband. He had left her at a time in her life when she felt vulnerable and confused. Richard's mother also felt tremendously guilty and ashamed for what Richard had done to her granddaughter. This had created a rift between her and her daughter which was slow to close. Also, Richard's mother had to confront the fact that her daughter was probably chemically dependent too.

Richard's prospects for a successful recovery were bleak, given all the contributing problems. Follow-up counseling would be long-term, and keeping this family involved was critical. It was imperative that Richard and I set goals which were achievable for him. Progress would be slow, but if I kept in mind his capacities, we could hopefully complete each goal.

Should teenagers attend AA meetings?

Alcoholics Anonymous can be very helpful to adolescents, but it may not be helpful to some. It is important to match the needs of the adolescent to the program, and AA is certainly a plausible alternative.

For the abusing adolescent, AA can provide information in an intense and direct manner. Few abusing adolescents have ever thanked me for sending them to AA, nor said they liked it. I did not send these kids because I thought they'd have a good time. I sent them because I felt they were open enough to be impacted by the meetings and would learn something about alcoholism. But, the adolescent must be mature enough to benefit from such an experience.

Early adolescents do not tend to do well at AA meetings; they find the experience too threatening. Also, early adolescents believe what they hear at AA meetings to be irrelevant to them. There are few AA meetings for children under the age of 14. However, if this age group were to benefit from AA, then they would do so in a homegeneous group, the same age. The abusing adolescent may need a different kind of educational experience than AA. AA meetings are not always "educational," and the abusing adolescent may do better at an alcohol/drug education class.

In most cases, the truly dependent youth should become involved in AA. The drug-addicted adolescent is in need of a new, drug-free peer group. Also, these kids do best in recovery when they are regularly reminded by their peers that they can no longer use drugs. This works best for the middle and late stage of adolescents. Early adolescents (11-14 years) still do not do particularly well in AA. Even if these kids are truly dependent, they generally have a hard time internalizing the values of the AA group. Intensive, ongoing family and individual counseling are usually better approaches.

As was mentioned earlier, Richard desperately needed AA to stay sober and out of trouble. As a result, Richard's sponsor required Richard to attend meetings every night. At first I agreed with this idea. But, as time went by, I could see that Richard was getting tired of AA, and was not developing in other areas of his life. I had seen this happen before, the adolescent would "burn out" on AA and want to get away from it. However, the adolescent would also feel guilty for not wanting to go to meetings. And so, these kids would just stop going to meetings. They did not feel confident enough to say to their sponsors, "I need to back off on so many meetings, it's just too much." I could see this coming for Richard.

It was therefore important to back Richard off of so many meetings and get him involved in some other activities. Just staying home once in a while was not a bad idea either. I did not want Richard's guilt over AA to undermine his sobriety. So Richard went to only three meetings a week and this helped. There was still some time for Richard to learn about what normal adolescents do.

How can younger siblings be prevented from becoming dependent also?

Younger siblings who watch their older brother, or sister get high are at risk to get into trouble themselves. One way to prevent this is to get the entire family involved in therapy as soon as possible. Also, the family should be encouraged to have family discussions about drug abuse. The parents need to convey clear messages to all their children regarding what they believe about alcohol and drug use for kids.

Can chemically dependent adolescents ever learn to be social users of alcohol and drugs?

Some follow-up studies have shown that a very few recovering adolescents have been able to start drinking again without any apparent problems. But, the reader should be cautioned to realize that these numbers are very small. In some cases, the dependency was related to a developmental disorder which eventually passed. In late adolescence these kids began to consume alcohol again and were able to drink in a controlled fashion. Generally, it is never recommended that a chemically dependent adolescent ever attempt to use any mood altering substance again. However, they will, and slips are common with recovering adolescents. Counselors should be prepared for these slips and not necessarily interpret them as failures.

The drug-abusing population is also advised to not try drinking at all, or at least until they reach the legal age. Often, the abusing child will eventually gain enough maturity that he may be able to drink socially.

Parental attitude is an important factor regarding this issue. If the parents agree that their child should be able to drink socially, then that child will probably try it. The counselor should work hard to teach the parents to hold the line on no teenage drug or alcohol use. It can be very harmful to the adolescent if their parents are ambivalent about this issue.

When should an adolescent and/or his family return for counseling?

Even when the counselors and the family feel they are finished with counseling they may not in fact be finished. This is why it is a good idea to discuss with the family and the adolescent potential conditions which might require them to return to counseling. A return to counseling may be precipitated by:

1. A perceived need by one, or all members of the family.
2. Some traumatic event like a slip, a divorce, a death, someone moves out of the house, an illness.
3. The identified patient begins to experience repeated failures.
4. Another member of the family begins to have problems, acts out.

In Richard's case, he and his mother agreed to return to counseling if he should stop going to AA, start using again, experience difficulty in controlling his sexual urges, wanted to move out of the house, or ever became violent.

How and why should a counselor cooperate with other agencies?

It is common for chemical dependency counselors to interact with juvenile courts, social caseworkers, school personnel and other counselors on a regular basis. When an adolescent is referred to you by an outside agency, it is best to respect their concerns and expectations. This is advisable, even when you believe the other agency is incorrect in their assessment of the adolescent.

Although it is best to respect and appreciate the other's point of view, it is never a good idea to allow them to dictate how to do therapy. You must make your own decisions on how to proceed with each individual case.

Social caseworkers usually have only the welfare of the individual adolescent in mind, and may even take an adversary role with the family. As a counselor, you definitely do not want to align yourself too closely with the caseworker. This could clearly sabotage any efforts to help the family.

Foster care workers tend to take a position similar to the social caseworkers in their interest for the adolescent. However, the foster care worker wil serve more of an intermediary role between the natural parents, the foster care parents and the child. It is often important for the counselor to work closely with the foster care worker in order to schedule appointments. Also, it is valuable to have opportunities to talk with the foster parents to understand what life is like in their home. And, in some situations, the counselor may want to get everyone together for an extended family counseling session.

Probation officers generally have final word on what is going to happen in a probationer's life. Having their cooperation is essential. However, probation officers may be so overloaded with cases that they do not follow each case closely. It is often true that the counselor will have a free hand with an adolescent, because the probation officer is busy with other cases. The attitude of the P.O. can be either positive or negative regarding your client. When there is a pessimistic attitude on the part of the P.O., it is best to distance yourself from him as tactfully as you can.

Sometimes, as a child gets caught up in all these service systems, the parents can end up receiving poor treatment. The parents may need an advocate who supports them and tries to help reinstate them as authorities in their family. It usually falls upon the counselor to do this.

Richard's mother possessed a particularly pessimistic attitude towards all the agents who were interfering in her life. She had good cause to feel this way. Since her son's arrest, she had come in contact with the police, a juvenile judge, two probation officers, the inpatient treatment staff, the halfway house staff, a social caseworker, a child protective service officer, an aftercare counselor and me.

This woman felt as if she had no more privacy, and her life was everybody's business. It took some time to win her over so she could put some confidence in me. At first she was resistant to more therapy, and so I had to empathize with her situation and not confront her. Eventually she came to value my opinion. This alliance was pivotal to the eventual success of Richard's recovery.

Richard and his mother came to an understanding of each other, and even began to depend upon each other for support. As therapy neared its end, I began to help both of them address future goals as independent people. Richard eventually found another job and left home. Richard's mother came to see her son as a competent adult and began to re-evaluate her future as a single person.

BIBLIOGRAPHY

Adelson, Joseph. *Handbook of Adolescent Psychology.* Wiley, 1980.

American Psychiatric Association. *Diagnostic and Statistical Manual of Mental Disorders:* Third Edition. APA: Washington, D.C., 1980.

Baumrind, D. Early socialization and adolescent competence. In, S. Dragastin, & G.H. Elder, (eds.), *Adolescence in the life cycle: Psychological change and social context.* New York: Wiley, 1975.

Berzonsky, M.D. Formal Reasoning in Adolescence: An Alternative View. *Adolescence,* No. 50, Summer, 1978.

Blos, P. *On Adolescence: A Psychoanalytic Interpretation.* New York: Free Press, 1962.

Blos, P. The second individuation process of adolescence. *Psychoanal. Study Child,* 22:162, 1967.

Coleman, A. How to enlist the family as an ally. *Am. J. Drug Abuse,* 3 (1), 1976.

Coleman, J.S., Bremmer, R.H., Burton, C.R., Davis, J.B., Eichorn, D.A., Grilches, Z., Kent, J.F., Ryder, N.B., Doering, Z.B., & Mays, I.M. *Youth: Transition to Adulthood.* Chicago: University of Chicago Press, 1974.

Daugherty, R., Neuman, D. and O'Brien, T. *Talking With Your Kids About Alcohol.* Prevention Research Institute: Lexington, KY.

Dufrense, J. & Cross, J.H. Personality variables in student drug use. Unpublished Master's Thesis, University of Connecticut, 1972.

Egan, M. Treatment of drug abuse. In, *Emotional Disorders in Children and Adolescents,* Sholevar, G.P. (ed.). Spectrum, 1980.

Elder, G. Structural variations in the child-rearing relationship. *Sociometry* 25:241-267, 1962.

Elder, G. Parental power legitimation and its effects. *Sociometry* 26:50-65, 1963.

Elkin, M. *Families Under the Influence: Changing Alcoholic Patterns.* Norton, 1984.

Elkind, D. Egocentrism in adolescence. *Child Development,* Vol. 38, 1967

Elkind, D. Understanding the young adolescent. *Adolescence.* Vol. XIII, No. 49, Spring, 1978.

Elkind, D. *The Hurried Child: Growing Up Too Fast, Too Soon.* Addison Wesley, 1981.

Ellis, D. Parents as participants, potential agents of change: Treatment for adolescent chemical dependency. *FOCUS On Family & Chemical Dependency,* Vol. 7, No. 5, 1984.

Ellis, D. When strategies fail. *J. of Systematic and Strategic Therapy.* 1986 (In press).

Enright, T., Lapsey, R., Drivas, O. & Fehr, G. Parental influences on the development of adolescent autonomy and identity. *J. of Youth and Adolescence,* Vol. 9, No. 6, 1980.

Erickson, E. *Childhood and Society.* New York: Norton, 1968.

Evans, John. *Adolescent and Pre-Adolescent Psychiatry.* Grune and Stratton, 1982.

Feather, N. Values in adolescence. In, *Handbook of Adolescent Psychology,* J. Adelson (ed.), New York: Wiley, 1980.

Feinstein, S.C. *Adolescence: Perspectives on Psychotherapy.* Jossey-Bass, 1980.

Forrest, G. *How To Cope With A Teenage Drinker.* Fawcett Crest, New York, 1983.

Handel, A. Perceived change of self among adolescents. *J. of Youth and Adolescence,* Vol. 9, No. 6, December, 1980.

Hoffman, L.W. Moral development in adolescents. In, *Handbook of Adolescent Psychology,* J. Adelson (ed.). Wiley, 1980.

Jones, M., & Bayley, N. Physical maturing among boys as related to behavior. *J. of Educational Psychology,* 41, 129-148, 1950.

Jordon, D. Parental antecendents of ego identity formation. Unpublished Master's Thesis, SUNY, at Brooklyn, 1970.

Jordon, D. Parental antecedents and personality characteristics of ego identity statuses. Unpublished doctoral dissertation, SUNY, at Brooklyn, 1971.

Josselson, R. Ego development in adolescence. In, *Handbook of Adolescent Psychology,* J. Adelson (ed.). Wiley, 1980.

Jurich, A., Polson, C., Jurich, J., Bates, R. Family factors in the lives of drug users and abusers. *Adolescence,* Vol. XX, No. 77, Spring, 1985.

Kolb, J. & Shapiro, E. Management of separation issues with the family of the hospitalized adolescent. In, *Adolescent Psychiatry: Developmental and Clinical Studies.* Fernstein, S.C. & Giovacchini, P. (eds.). Vol.8, University of Chicago Press: Chicago-London, 1982.

Klinge, V., Laschar, D., Grisell, J. & Berman, W. Effects of scoring norms on adolescent psychiatric drug abusers and non-users MMPI profiles. *Adolescence,* Vol. XIII, No. 49, Spring, 1978.

Lawson, G., Ellis, D. & Rivers, C. *Essentials of Chemical Dependency Counseling.* Aspen Systems, 1984.

Logan, R. A re-conceptualization of Erickson's identity stage. *Adolescence.* Vol, XVIII, No. 72, Winter, 1983.

McAuliffe, R.M. & McAuliffe, M.B. *Essentials for the Diagnosis of Chemical Dependency.* Minneapolis, Minn: The Am. Chemical Dependency Society, 1975.

Marcia, J.E. Ego identity status: Relationship to change in self-esteem, "general misadjustment," and authoritarianism. *J. of Personality,* 35 (1), 119-133, 1967.

Marcia, J. Identity in adolescence. In, *Handbook of Adolescent Psychology.* J. Adelson (ed.). New York: Wiley, 1980.

Materson, J. *The Psychiatric Dilemma of Adolescence.* Boston: Little Brown, 1967.

Materson, J. The psychiatric significance of adolescent turmoil. *Am. J. of Psychiatry,* 124, 1549-1554, 1968.

Materson, J. *Treatment of the Borderline Adolescent: A Developmental Approach.* New York: Wiley-Interscience, 1972.

Meeks, J.E. *The Fragile Alliance; An Orientation to the Outpatient Psychotherapy of the Adolescent.* Williams and Wilkins, Baltimore, 1971.

Offer, D. *The Psychological World of the Teenager.* New York: Basic Books, 1969.

Offer, D. & Offer, J. Normal adolescence in perspective. In, *Current Issues in Adolescent Psychiatry,* Schoolar, J. (ed.). Brunner and Mazel, 1973.

Offer, D. & Offer J. *From Teenage to Young Manhood.* New York: Basic Books, 1975.

Owen, P.L., Nyberg, R.L. Assessing alcohol and drug problems among adolescents: Current Practices. *J. Drug Education,* Vol. 13 (3), 1983.

Peele, S. *Don't Panic: A Parents Guide to Understanding and Preventing Alcohol and Drug Abuse.* CompCare, 1983.

Peskin, H. & Livson, N. Pre and postpuberty personality and adult psychologic functioning. *Seminars in Psychiatry,* 4, 343-354, 1972.

Piaget, J. *Psychology of Intelligence.* London: Keagan Paul, 1950.

Poley, W., Lea, G. & Vibe, G. *Alcoholism: A Treatment Manual.* N.Y.: Gardner Press, 1979.

Reardon, B. & Griffing, P. Factors related to the self-concept of institutionalized, White male adolescent drug abusers. *Adolescence,* Vol. XVIII, No. 69, Spring, 1983.

Ritterman, M. *Using Hypnosis in Family Therapy.* Jossey-Bass, 1983.

Roberts, R. Treating conduct disordered adolescents and young adults by working with the parents. *J. of Marriage and Family Therapy,* January, 1982.

Rokeach, M. *The Nature of Human Values.* New York: Free Press, 1973.

Schoolar, J. *Current Issues in Adolescent Psychiatry.* Brunner-Mazel, 1973.

Shapiro, R. A family therapy approach to alcoholism. *J. of Marriage and Family Counseling,* October, 1977.

Shapiro, R. Family therapy with children and adolescents: Psychodynamic approaches. In, *Treatment of Emotional Disorders in Children and Adolescents,* Sholevar, R., Benson, M. & Blinder, B. (eds.). New York: Spectrum, 1978.

Schilling, K.L. Ego identity status: A re-evaluation and extension of construct validity. Unpublished doctoral dissertation, University of Florida, 1975.

Staton, M.D. & Todd, T.C. Structural family therapy with drug addicts. In, *The Family Therapy of Drug and Alcohol Abuse,* E. Kaufman & P. Kaufman, (eds.). New York: Gardner Press, 1979.

Stanton, M.D., Todd, T.C. & Assoc. *The Family Therapy of Drug Abuse and Addiction.* New York: Guilford, 1982.

Steinberg, D. *Clinical Psychiatry of Adolescence: An Approach to Diagnosis.* Wiley Interscience, New York, 1983.

Toffler, A. *The Third Wave.* Bantam, 1980.

Wegscheider, S. *Another Chance: Hope and Health for the Alcoholic Family.* Science and Behavior, 1981.

Weissman, S. Strategies for individual or family therapy of adolescence. In, *Adolescence, Perspectives on Psychotherapy,* Feinstein, S. (ed.). Jossey-Bass, 1980.